2004 POET

ONCE UPON A RHYME

IMAGINATION FOR
A NEW GENERATION

South Hampshire
Edited by Natalie Catterick

 Young**Writers**

First published in Great Britain in 2004 by:
Young Writers
Remus House
Coltsfoot Drive
Peterborough
PE2 9JX
Telephone: 01733 890066
Website: www.youngwriters.co.uk

SB ISBN 1 84460 507 8

Foreword

Young Writers was established in 1991 and has been passionately devoted to the promotion of reading and writing in children and young adults ever since. The quest continues today. Young Writers remains as committed to engendering the fostering of burgeoning poetic and literary talent as ever.

This year's Young Writers competition has proven as vibrant and dynamic as ever and we are delighted to present a showcase of the best poetry from across the UK. Each poem has been carefully selected from a wealth of *Once Upon A Rhyme* entries before ultimately being published in this, our twelfth primary school poetry series.

Once again, we have been supremely impressed by the overall high quality of the entries we have received. The imagination, energy and creativity which has gone into each young writer's entry made choosing the best poems a challenging and often difficult but ultimately hugely rewarding task - the general high standard of the work submitted amply vindicating this opportunity to bring their poetry to a larger appreciative audience.

We sincerely hope you are pleased with our final selection and that you will enjoy *Once Upon A Rhyme South Hampshire* for many years to come.

Contents

Hannah Kennedy (9)	19
Edward Newbold (7)	20
Loren Ockelford (10)	20
Amy Burglin (11)	20
Hannah Cole (11)	21
Kia Hancock (11)	21
Colette Hayes (10)	22
Gemma Johnstone (11)	22
Bethany Scourfield (11)	23
Christopher Chester-Sterne (10)	23
Paul Alp (11)	24
Stephanie Clark (10)	24
Molly Brimson (7)	25
Ryan O'Connor (8)	25
Carmen Green (10)	26
Declan Irvine (10)	26
Thomas Church (11)	27
Monica Morton (11)	27
Reuben Adam Capstick (8)	28
Christine Hughes (8)	29
Sophie Bunday (10)	29
Charlotte Pilcher (11)	30
Zoe Hanley (11)	30
Marie Atkinson (10)	31
Charlotte Willbourne (10)	31
Mark Stevens (10)	32
Laura Vincent (8)	32
Matthew Amess (10)	33
Daryl Price (11)	33
Emma Tregarthen (9)	34
Shaun Rollinson (10)	34
Emma Brown (10)	35
Grant Adlem (10)	35
Joshua Capstick (10)	36
Sasha Hutton (11)	37
Holly Kinggett (10)	37

Calmore Junior School

Aimee Paddick (10)	38
Daniel Cornick (10)	38
Philip Hemborough (10)	39

Harrison Primary School

Newbridge Junior School

Bracken Pluckrose (10)	59
Bethany Goodchild (10)	60
Rosie Robertson (10)	60
Amber Jane Privett (9)	61
Lauren Dewhurst (9)	62
Daniel Belstone (11)	63
Georgina Anne Nicholls (10)	64
Harvey Scott-Cooper (10)	65
Yasmin Wells (10)	66
Toby Walton (9)	66
Jackson Ball (11)	67
Joseph Quinlan (9)	67
Emily Tann (11)	68
Ashleigh Muns (11)	69
Andrew Bentley (10)	70
Claire Norman (11)	71
Shane Filleul (11)	71
Kim Allison (11)	72
Harriet Standen (10)	73
Chelsea Kellett (10)	74
Jake Lawrence (10)	75
Katie-May Firth (10)	76
Cally Surman (11)	77
Natalie King (11)	78

North Baddesley Junior School

Bethany Meredith (11)	78
Emma Whitty (10)	79
Stephanie White (11)	79
Charlotte Ashworth (10)	79
Natalie Harris (11)	80
Sammie Whitty (10)	80

Red Barn Primary School

Curtis Sanderson (10)	81
Christopher Kelly (10)	81
Thomas Guildford (9)	82
Adam Spencer-Hicken (9)	83
Nathan Huitson (9)	84
Bradley Elmes (10)	84
Adam Long (11)	84

Blake Folgado (10)	85
Connor Blyth (9)	85
Samuel Wickham (9)	85
Keith Edwards (11)	86
Annabelle Phelan (11)	86
Megan Standen (11)	87
Benjamin Davis (11)	88
Elliot Elcock (10)	88
Ann-Marie Hinshelwood (9)	88
Emily Seall (11)	89
James Goble (10)	89
Joseph Rinomhota (8)	89
Charlie Anderson (11)	90
Ryan Burrows (10)	91
Kirsty Lloyd (11)	91
Maisie Chambers (10)	92
Roxanne Reeve (11)	92
Georgia-Mae Holloway (8)	93
Connor Phipps (10)	93
Lincoln Pepall (9)	94
James Payne (9)	94
Connor Morrison (8) & Tom Webb (9)	94
Kathryn Booth (9)	95
Connor Waring (9)	96
Nicole Mattravers (9)	96
Ronny Chambers (9)	96
Carla Huitson (9)	97
Jay Wake (8)	97
James Milner (9)	97
Rebecca Masterson (11)	98

St Anthony's Catholic Primary School, Fareham

Ashley Hyde (9)	98
Emily Zambra (9)	99
Abigail Prosser (9)	100
Christian Davison (8)	101
Conor Hurren (9)	102
Lucy Markham (8)	103
Lauren Andrews (8)	104
William Fairman (8)	105
Bethany Woolford (9)	106

Rachel Giles (8)   107
Zach Johnston (9)   108
Amelia Notley (8)   109
Freya Evershed (8)   110
Charlotte Stanton (8)   111
Charlie Briant (9)   112
Shauna Solomon (9)   113
Jordan Stanley (9)   114
James Wallis (9)   114
William Piper (9)   115

St Paul's Catholic Primary School, Portsmouth
Millie Manchip (8)   116
Megan Holt (8)   116
Tanya Bee (9)   117
Charlotte Smith (9)   117
Callum Ardern (9)   117
Tom Smith (9)   118
Brett Togwell (8)   118
Callum Veale (9)   119
Charlie Cooper (9)   120
Jessica Warren (8)   120
Holly Duckett (8)   120
Sarrah Agulan (9) & Jack Wilkes (10)   121
Kevin Johnson (8)   121
Lucy Catterall (9)   122
Sean Burby (10) & Carmen Langworthy (10)   123
Shelby Chitwood (10) & Lloyd Conner (9)   124

St Swithun's RC Primary School, Southsea
Niall Anderson (10)   124
Brendan Keegan (10)   125
Jessica Moore (11)   125
Victoria Hopkins (10)   126
Lucy Hennigan (11)   126
Charlie John Gardener (10)   127
Victoria Reeves (10)   127
Katie Jones (10)   128
Charlotte Tait (11)   128
Elisabeth Sarah Welfare (10)   129
Patrick Symonds (10)   129

Misha Sugrue-Gee (11)   130
Clay Thompson (11)   130
Aden Thomas Flannagan (10)   130

The Crescent Primary School
Olivia Wood (9)   131
Laura Newman (8)   131
Charmaine Ivermee (8)   132
Callum Moore (8)   132
Zoe Handley-Greaves (8)   133
Krissy Donohue (9)   133
Shaneece Waller Adams (8)   134
Abbie Marie Humphries (8)   134
Thomas Dodson (9)   135
Daniel Cardinal (9)   135
Stephen Coles (8)   136
Elizabeth Wyatt (9)   136
Luke Blackburn (9)   137
Maisie James (8)   137
Abigail Wright (8)   138
Lorna Collins (8)   138
Samantha Tait (9)   139
Shireena Frederick (8)   139
Madeleine Hobbs (9)   140
Abbie Stevens (8)   140
Kanesha Agard (8)   141
Emma Baxter (8)   141
Jake Herbert Peatroy (8)   141
Lottie Jarvis (8)   142
Nicole Watson (9)   142
Tyler Rossi (8)   143
Jack Ibbs (9)   143
Jamie Edwards (9)   144
Samantha Walls (9)   144
Ben Tyrrell (8)   145
Benjamin Whiteside (9)   145
Robert Jones (8)   146
Lauren Andrews (8)   146
Amy Burley (9)   147
Daniel Flux (9)   147
Sam Broadhurst (9)   148

Katie Humphreys (8)   148
Madeleine June Kenrick (8)   149
Hayley Kellaway (8)   149
Nick Chan (9)   150
Michael Turner (8)   150
Kim Lloyd (8)   151
Charlie White (8)   151

Wallop CP School
Toby Hudson (10)   152
Emma Hodges (10)   152
Harry Blackburn (10)   152
Amy Donald (11)   153
Joseph Day (10)   153
Emily Whordley (10)   153
Adam Bate (11)   154
Ashley Baxter (11)   154
Annabel Dahne (9)   155
Anna Hibberd (7)   155
Cecilia King (10)   156
Jessica Fenton (11)   156
Katherine Shadwell (11)   156
Christopher Gallop (11)   157
Chloe Wood (10)   157
Andrew Brotherwood (11)   158
Jack Brown (7)   158
Jessica Malcolm (10)   158
Robin Cook (11)   159
James Scott (8)   159
Kieron Grist (11) & Andrew   159
Alexandra Bryony Sears (7)   160
Kate O'Brien (10)   160
Emma Sophie Blackburn (8)   161
Rory Wood (7)   161
Christopher Burden (10)   162
Kara Hind (7)   162
Sophie Johnson (10)   162
Jason Dibble (10)   163
Luke Bulpitt (11)   163
Oliver Yates & Adam Bate (11)   163

Wildground Junior School

Lauren Wood (11)	164
Stephanie Randell (11)	164
Josie Myers (8)	165
Kailey Hole (11)	165
Nicole Perry (11)	166
Laura Thurston (8)	166
Holly Penny (9)	166
Ellen Powell (10)	167
Jessica Maunder (9)	167
Bethany Hibberd (10)	168
Shannen Sultana (10)	168
Michael Quinn (8)	169
Chelsea Penny (10)	170
Rebecca Mole (11)	170
Amy Benham (11)	170
Ben Fusedale (7)	171
Eleanor Watson (8)	171
Catherine Hoare (11)	171
Catriona O'Brien (8)	172
Louise Holloway (9)	172

The Poems

Ghosts

In the shadows, great and small
Ghosts appearing on the wall
Screeching, screaming through the night
Giving you a massive fright

Ghosts are coming
Coming to you
Ghosts are coming
Shouting, *'Boo!'*

In the dead of night they're there
Upsetting you, but they don't care
Floating up high in the sky
They're never hurt, they never die

Ghosts are coming
Coming to you
Ghosts are coming
Shouting, *'Boo!'*

Nicola Horrobin (11)
Beechwood Junior School

Snow

A white blanket of snow covers the ground,
The world is still, not even a sound,
Soft, feathery flakes fall from the sky,
Swirling, dancing, watch them fly.

See the children dressed in coats and gloves,
Snowballs whizzing like startled doves,
A snowman stands with a carrot nose,
He'll stay as long as the north wind blows.

Laura Price (11)
Beechwood Junior School

My Hamster

I have a little hamster
Who is a happy chap,
And when I get him out to play
He sits upon my lap.

But sometimes when I look away
And he goes to find his food,
When he puts it in his mouth
It looks extremely rude.

When I get back from school
To see if he is there,
He pops down from his tube and looks
Just like a ball of hair.

When he runs around his wheel
The odd four hundred times,
He feels as though he wants a meal
And that he's in his prime.

Gus Aspden (11)
Beechwood Junior School

Mighty Dragon

He's known for vicious slaying,
His yellow teeth covered in blood.
Skeletons lay like logs at his feet,
Long sharp claws for ripping flesh.
His eyes glow like red rubies.
His spiky tail hovering behind
Skin rough as sandpaper.
Puffs of grey smoke emerge from his nostrils,
Trees fall like dominoes in his path.
The mighty dragon thunders towards the village.

Danielle Robinson (10)
Beechwood Junior School

Winter

Rain comes down in a heavy fall,
Splattering everywhere and getting you soaked.
Shivery and cold you snuggle up by the fire,
Then run yourself a hot bath filled with white pure bubbles.

Winter, winter don't bother me!
Winter, winter, just do your thing!

Snow and ice,
Frost and rain.
All fall down but I don't care,
Cos I'm in the warm, all snug and cuddly,
I'll just wait until this weather goes away.

Winter, winter, don't bother me!
Winter, winter, just do your thing!

Letitia Layton (11)
Beechwood Junior School

TV

TV is the ultimate entertainer,
From all corners of life.
Soaps and cartoons entertain,
Sitcoms make you laugh.
Adverts annoy you,
Documentaries and the News
Teach and inform you,
Shopping saves your legs,
DIY and cooking gives you new ideas.
See and hear the whole world,
Through this wondrous box.

Harry French (11)
Beechwood Junior School

Hamsters

Hamsters are cute,
Hamsters are quick,
My hamster is quiet,
But likes to do the odd trick.

Hamsters are sweet,
Hamsters are small,
My hamster is fluffy,
But definitely not tall.

Hamsters are scruffy,
Hamsters are neat,
My hamster fights others,
Whenever they meet.

My hamster stores food
In both of its cheeks.
On the odd occasion
I give him some treats.

My hamster is special,
I love him to bits,
Even when he keeps me awake
Doing late night tricks!

Jessica Jennings (11)
Beechwood Junior School

Nothing

On a dark, dark night
Along a dark, dark lane,
There was a dark, dark house
And in that dark, dark, house,
There was a dark, dark room
And in that dark, dark room
There was a dark, dark chest,
And in that dark, dark chest
There was *nothing!*

Shannen Birks (11)
Beechwood Junior School

Winter

When it is winter,
You should wear lots of thick clothing
This will keep you nice and warm,
And it will when it's snowing.

Wintertime is going soon,
What a great relief
Everyone is happy now
There'll be no more chattering teeth.

No more cold wintry nights,
What a happy thought
I'll miss snuggling up to my family,
I won't need the gloves I brought

When winter is past,
It will be so much better
Spring will be here and
Without shaking, I can write a letter.

Now spring is coming,
Which will be great
Lots more warmer weather,
So you can play outside with your mate.

Kayleigh Brown (10)
Beechwood Junior School

Silent Snow

Snowflakes falling all around,
Hits the ground, not even a sound.
The ice has broken, the snow has fallen,
The day has woken, it froze the bell.
The snowballs come from size to size,
Have a snowman competition, you may win a prize.
The snowman stands, the sun is out,
The sun has come, to snow land,
There's no sound about.

Rebecca Gooch (10)
Beechwood Junior School

Elephant

Slowly swaying this way and that,
The elephant guides his way,
Through the sandy scenes so smooth and flat,
It really can take all day!

See how he pauses to take a rest,
And calmly flaps his ears.
Carefully deciding which path is best,
And the noises of animals he hears.

The lion with his paws out,
Snores softly as he sleeps,
The giraffe is awake and about,
And from behind her, her baby peeps.

But the elephant settles down,
To dream of the next day,
To travel to the town,
Of where the animals play!

Rosie Jayne Paton (10)
Beechwood Junior School

Chocolate

There was a young girl called Bethany,
Who loved all things chocolatey,
She ate such a lot
Thin, she was not.
Her friends said, 'Oh Beth, you're all wobbly.'

True, chocolate can make you wobble
And get you into trouble,
If you eat it too quick
It can make you feel sick,
But it's so very nice, I'll have double!

Beth Broadbent (11)
Beechwood Junior School

In And Out Of A Winter's Day

Morning:
A carpet of snow glistened
Under the morning sun.
First light filtered across the land,
Day has just begun.

Young ones wake and see the snow,
Their faces are bright and cheerful.
They run out to play and slip,
Their expressions change to tearful.

Midday:
The sun is high up in the sky,
Its warm rays spread around.
Field mice sleep inside their nests,
Everything is sound.

Cats curled up, asleep on the bed,
Enjoying the warmth and heat.
Their furry chests gently rise,
The cold weather, they will beat.

Evening:
Snow gently falls onto the rooftop,
And the wind cuts through the trees like blades.
Cats scratch at the door to be let in
As the sun fades.

Children sit around the fire,
The fire is welcoming and bright.
Red and yellow, its flames flicker,
It warms up the lonely night.

Bianca Collings (10)
Beechwood Junior School

If I Had Wings

If I had wings I would
Fly to the Trifle Tower
And eat it, layer by layer.

If I had wings I would
Fly to the Empire Cake Building
And eat it, level by level.

If I had wings I would
Fly to the top of the London Pie
And eat it,
Seat by seat.

If I had wings I would
Fly to the Big Hen
And eat it,
Number by number.

If I had wings I would
Fly to the Coliseum
And eat it
Row by row.

If I had wings I would
Fly to the Leaning Tower of Pizza
And eat it
Crust by crust.

If I had wings I would
Fly to the Bucket of Ham Palace
And eat it
Slice by slice.

If I had wings I would
Fly to the centre of Turkey
Smother it in gravy
And eat it piece by piece.

If I had wings I would
Fly to the Millennium Scone
And eat it
Filling by filling.

Ross Taylor (11)
Beechwood Junior School

The Evil Teacher

The evil teacher (that's what we call her)
Prancing around, wearing fake fur,
She gives us cold looks just like we don't care
She makes us feel stupid but we're unaware.

She wears a black wig that's tatty and old
She thinks we don't notice but we know she's bold,
She has long pointy feet that curl at the end
To chop off her feet, I would recommend.

She comes into school with a cauldron as a bag
A long black coat along with a name tag.
She's so scruffy (she can't be rich)
Oy yes, I've got it, she's a
Witch!

Millie Joseph (11)
Beechwood Junior School

Autumn Leaves

All the different coloured leaves
That fall from the autumn trees,
Swirling, turning everywhere
Flying through the frosty air.

Some are crumbled, some are plain
Slowly making a crispy chain.
The leaves leave the trees, all bold
So they can easily unfold.

When they reach the leafy ground,
They pile up without a sound.
Finally finished the journey through the sky
They lay down and die.

Elena Grubb (11)
Beechwood Junior School

Dolphins

Dolphins are the best
Better than the rest.
They soar up high and swoop down low,
That is the way a dolphin's life goes.
They like fish
But not on a dish,
They hum and not sing,
But they make the ocean sparkle like a diamond ring.
Dolphins are the best,
Better than the rest.

Dolphins are the best,
Better than the rest.
Dolphins glide through the sea,
They can hold their breath for 20 minutes, wow wee.
They have two fins and a tail and a tummy very pale.
Dolphins are the best,
Better than the rest.

Elena Gray (10)
Beechwood Junior School

Silly Sounding Poem

One wacky whale whipped weird wombats,
Two tiny toes threw timid tigers,
Three thin things thundered through the thicket,
Four fearsome fleas fought funny ferrets,
Five female felines fight for food,
Six slithering snakes slap silly snails.
Seven strange sea lion swim seven seas,
Eight enormous elephants eat excellent eggs,
Nine naughty nightingales nibbled nasty nuts,
Ten terrible toads teased terrified tadpoles.

Lewis Whitlock (11)
Beechwood Junior School

Midnight

The streets are empty and dark,
And no one is around,
The swings are silent in the park,
Is that what happens when it's dark?

The children are tucked up in their beds,
Having sweet dreams,
The eerie silence of the street
It's not quite what it seems.

The stars are shimmering in the sky,
The moon is shining bright.
The birds are climbing in their nest
The cats are out tonight.

From the corner of my eye,
A shadow appears,
I put my head beneath the sheet,
And try to hide my fears.

I don't know what time it is,
Must be about midnight.
Better get to sleep now,
Can't wait until it's light.

Sasha John (10)
Beechwood Junior School

Happiness

Happiness is the summer holidays,
Happiness is a brand new top,
Happiness is the sunshine shining bright,
Happiness is a pair of brand new boots.
Happiness is a shining bike,
Happiness is a gleaming present,
Happiness is having a baby.
Happiness is a new teacher,
Happiness is having a birthday.

Kerry Etheridge (8)
Blackfield Junior School

Christmas

C is for carollers, singing in the cold,
H is for holly on the door.
R is for reindeer, flying in the sky
I is for icicles hanging from the roof.
S is for snow on the ground,
T is for turkey on the table.
M is for mince pies which Santa eats
A is for Advent Calendar
S is for Santa, coming down the chimney.

Rebecca White (9)
Blackfield Junior School

Poem

A dventure, adventure always an adventure
D own in a valley or up on a mountain
V alleys and mountains surround the sea
E verywhere is always an adventure
N ever without an adventure
T errifying castles or beautiful gardens
U nder big rocks or in a cave
R eady, I'm ready. Are you ready for an adventure?
E verywhere always with an adventure.

Sidney Baldwin (7)
Blackfield Junior School

Party

P resents in the cupboard
A ngel cake, waiting to be eaten.
R unning children with new toys,
T iny Tible tiptoeing around
Y o-yos bouncing up and down
S oft toys lying on the ground.

Sophie Burt (8)
Blackfield Junior School

Stage Life

For weeks I've been practising,
I know all my steps by heart,
But still I'm very nervous,
As the panto music starts.

The curtains open, the lights go up,
I'm waiting in the wings,
Ready to dance across the stage,
As an actress loudly sings.

I swallow hard and on I go,
I hope I don't fall down,
The theatre's full of paying guests,
Who've travelled into town.

This is my perfect moment,
Though it only lasts a while,
Tummy in, head up and dance,
And don't forget to smile.

My nerves have gone, I'm having fun,
As music fills the air,
For now I am a theatre star,
Dancing without a care.

That's it, the end, I've done it,
I'm feeling great right now,
Cheers, flowers and clapping,
As I take my final bow.

Alice Liddon (11)
Blackfield Junior School

Winter

Winter is a deep blue snowy night where the sleet
is trickling down. As the dark sky darkens, I stand
by the fire and wish it was summer.
Outside the tall trees blow in the wind with
a whooshing sound which gives you a fright.

Stephanie Warne (9)
Blackfield Junior School

Dancing

I put on my soft satin shoes
And then my pink leotard
We get to class and dance and dance
The lessons are really hard.

Competitions are really great
I like to go with my best mate
She always is really funny
We love to go and spend our money.

Our teacher shouts, really loud
She can scare a massive crowd
Sometimes she shouts at me
To make me jump as high as a tree.

We dance all night and we dance all day
We never have the time to play
We love to jump and we love to skip
Because we don't feel like we're under the whip!

When I'm older, it will be my job
If I don't get in, I will start to sob
Next year I will try my best
I'm half-way through an important quest.

Amy Marzaroli (8)
Blackfield Junior School

Houses

If people were houses, I would be a flat because it is tall,
If my dad was a home, he would be a cottage because it's warm.
If my mum was a home, she would be a bungalow because it's small.
If my sister was a home, she would be a caravan because
She likes adventures.

Daniel Pilcher (8)
Blackfield Junior School

Wings

If I had wings
I would land on Mars and find life
And play with the man in the moon, 'Yeah!'

If I had wings
I would taste the rainbow, 'Yum!'
And find the pot of gold at the other end.

If I had wings
I would tell someone to get on my back
And I would fly them into space, 'Wee!'

If I had wings
I would jump on the sun, 'Hot, hot, very hot!'
And play on it all day long.

If I had wings
I would fly down to my bed
And fall straight to sleep, 'Night, night!'

Scott Hutchings (9)
Blackfield Junior School

The Little Frog

The little frog was tired and hot
So he thought, *I'll go to my favourite spot*
The little frog was very fond
Of diving into the lily pond
But when he dived, he couldn't stop
He went *boink!* instead of *plop!*
The little frog was quite amazed
And set in the little pond, quite dazed
All the water had gone away
But it had started to rain. Hip hip hooray.

Jordan Cotterill-Clark (8)
Blackfield Junior School

Winter

From the black sky of night
A white blanket covers the town
Everyone look out of the window
Snow is falling down!

Grab your coat grab your hat
Come out and play
Watch out a snowball is coming
Oh no you've been hit, there you lay.

Wake up wake up come inside
You've been knocked out
Are you alright?
What are you on about?

James Graham (10)
Blackfield Junior School

Crystals

Crystals, crystals, crystals,
How lovely do you shine?
I see you on the windowpane
Glittering wondrously fine.

You sparkle in the sunlight
And give me lots of lights,
You twinkle like the stars at night
And give me lots of delight.

Crystals, crystals, crystals,
How do you ever shine?
You sparkle every day and night,
Sitting in a line.

Hannah Morton (9)
Blackfield Junior School

Ballerina

A ballerina is graceful and talented,
They wear a leotard, tights and ballet shoes.
They wear their hair scraped back into a bun
And dance to entertain everyone.

The music they dance to is classical
Which has got violins, flute and a piano in it.
The ballerina has got special positions for her feet
They'll have different glides which go up and up,
They get harder as you move on.

A ballerina has to practise and rehearse,
They do shows on the stage at the end of every year.
They all dress up for their shows
As characters in fancy costumes.
Family and friends can come and see
To make them proud and happy.

Sadie Alexander (7)
Blackfield Junior School

Snow

It was late at night when it started to snow
From where it came, I do not know,
It was fluffy and light
And oh so bright
But made the world look a wonderful sight.

Children came out to run and play,
Before the snow all melted away.
It may be years before we see
The lovely snow that fell on me.

Erin Irvine (8)
Blackfield Junior School

The Cat

A cat is a lovely pet,
She has big blue eyes.
She moves very fast and quietly,
At night, she goes hunting mice,
With her shiny paws.
She lives in a small house.

I saw her in the garden,
She was playing with the beautiful flowers.
Suddenly, she saw a rat run past,
And she ran after it at top speed.
Afterwards she came in the garden,
She wanted to come indoors
And she wanted her food,
She is a very good girl, she never eats stealthily.

Papin Nguyen (10)
Blackfield Junior School

Unloved, Alone

U nloved and discarded
N obody cares,
L ove is what lived here
O ver the years.
V agrants do visit but
E veryone leaves
D ismissed out of mind.

A lifetime of misery,
L oved ones have left,
O h how it wishes its
N ightmare could end,
E ven now it trembles again . . .
    and longs for a family to bring
    it alive once again.

Jacob Sharpe
Blackfield Junior School

The River Otter

It's a playful time for the river otter,
In the spring's glorious shine,
It finds its food with its great long whiskers
As it dashes along the flowing stream.

The otter likes its freedom for now
It is not hunted for its glorious coat,
It's now protected all of the time.

The otter is a curious thing,
It watches the bank with its big brown eyes.
As soon as it sees its prey the tail comes into play,
With one big swish it darts away.

It talks in a squeaking way to all of the otters
To come and play.
Sliding down the mud banks, gliding all of the way.

It is a graceful creature and fun with it too,
So next time you see an otter just sit and view.

Hannah Dewey (10)
Blackfield Junior School

As We Whizzed Through The City

Faster than dogs, faster than cats,
As we whizzed passed the houses and passed the flats.
Across the bridges and across the road
Knocking the frogs and knocking the toads.

Flying through the traffic jams, flying through the city
Looking at all the litter, that's such a pity,
Children crying, children screaming,
As the sun was beaming.

Hannah Kennedy (9)
Blackfield Junior School

I'm Always On The Go!

I'm a seven year old boy
I'm always on the go!
I like to run around,
I'm always on the go!
I love to ride my bike, really fast.
I'm always on the go!
I enjoy going to the park,
I'm always on the go!
I'm every day, every second, *always on the go!*

Edward Newbold (7)
Blackfield Junior School

My Family

My family is so special to me
Especially my daddy.
I love my mummy just as much
But I need to tell you as such.
My mummy is very funny
And my daddy has a wobbly tummy.
They both wear brightly coloured socks
But forget that, my family rocks!

Loren Ockelford (10)
Blackfield Junior School

Pigeon

As evening falls and shadows fly
My eyes are fixed to a darkening sky
It is you feathered friend
That I await but darkness descends
And now it's too late.

Amy Burglin (11)
Blackfield Junior School

A Poem About Different Animals!

Monkeys have tails which swing this way and that,
The lion's mane is just like a hat!

A giraffe's neck can stretch to the treetop,
Rabbits don't walk, they jump and hop!

The blue dolphin leaps up out of the sea,
Black and yellow, the colours of a bee!

Tortoises carry their homes upon their back,
A kangaroo carries her baby tucked in her sack!

The tiger's stripes help her hide in the grass,
Bats sleep all day, and get up at dusk!

Animals are made of many different things,
From scales to feathers, from fur to wings!

Hannah Cole (11)
Blackfield Junior School

The Sun Is . . .

The sun is hot
The sun is warm
The sun is big
The sun is greater than you or me.
It shines in the puddles below the tree.
The sun is hot
The sun is warm
The sun is big
The sun is very, very bright.
You need sunglasses to shade your eyes from the light.
The sun is hot
The sun is warm
The sun is big
The sun has gone!

Kia Hancock (11)
Blackfield Junior School

Speedy My Giant Tortoise

Speedy is a herbivore and he likes to eat fruit, grass and leaves
But he doesn't like to weave
He doesn't have any teeth but he has a friend called Keith
So that Speedy can eat he has a mouth like a beak
And it's very hard not weak.

Speedy can grow as high as 76 centimetres
And grow as long as 180 centimetres
He can weigh more than 200 kilograms
Not 200 centimetres.

When Speedy gets frightened he pulls his head
And his legs into his shell
Without sounding like a bell.

Then the enemy can't get him and backs away
So Speedy can enjoy the rest of his day.

Colette Hayes (10)
Blackfield Junior School

Colours Of The Rainbow

White is soft snow falling gently.
Blue is the deep sea with dolphins swimming in it.
Yellow is the sun on a hot summer's day.
Pink is the sunset from a beautiful day.
Brown is a pig covered in mud.
Black is the dark night.
Gold is a smile from a happy child.
Silver is a diamond sparkling.
Red is a rose given to someone on Valentine's.
Orange is an orang-utan running round the zoo.
Green is the long grass growing really tall.
Purple is an octopus swimming through the sea.
Blue and white is the sea and the waves crashing against the rocks.
Pink and red is my heart that I keep for two special people,
My mum and dad!

Gemma Johnstone (11)
Blackfield Junior School

It's Snowing!

Jumping out from my warm and cosy bed,
I ran to the window and looked straight ahead.
The shining sun lit up the snow,
I quickly dressed, from head to toe.

Excitedly hauling open the door,
I bent down to scrape off the floor.
Freezing snowballs melting in my hands,
I started to make something really grand.

Piling up the snow into a great heap,
It started to look like a fluffy sheep.
In the end, it finally looked right,
I was really pleased with the amazing sight.

As I went in for a warm drink,
I looked in the mirror; my nose was all pink.
I stared out the window to admire the snow,
Perched on my snowman, was a little crow!

Bethany Scourfield (11)
Blackfield Junior School

The Monkey

Swinging through the jungle came a
Great big hairy monkey,
His arms were long, his fur was black
And his nose was rather wonky!

His friends and family came for dinner,
They dined on leaves and fruit
And afterwards they made their nests,
With moss and twigs and shoots.

He ate lots of yellow bananas,
They gave him a big round belly,
And if he sat right next to you,
You'd find he's very smelly!

Christopher Chester-Sterne (10)
Blackfield Junior School

Leopard's Prey

As the animals of the jungle move onto the open grass,
The leopard watches in starvation,
So he creeps up slowly,
The animals don't suspect a thing,
But they were wrong.

The herd closest was the antelope,
As he crept closer and closer,
The antelope sees the grass moving about,
One of the herd went up to the grass.
Without warning the leopard pounced.

Loudly it let out a cry,
As the other animals fled,
The leopard ate away,
Chewing away on the dead carcass the wife came
And the cubs did as well.

The family thought
This is enough to fill me for the day,
While the animals were over the other side of the land
Their other problem was cheetahs.

Paul Alp (11)
Blackfield Junior School

Snow

The white blanket covered the land,
It crunched beneath my feet,
Oh how I wished I could get up
From my snow angel and stand,
It made me want to get back in my bed
And hide under my sheet.

The snow even covered the window ledge,
The cold crisp air grabbed me like a vice,
I ran to get my sledge,
It was the scent that made you click it was winter.

Stephanie Clark (10)
Blackfield Junior School

The Fairy Clown

Here is a story about a fairy called Star
It's really quite funny but also bizarre
Now Star is the clumsiest fairy I know
From the top of her head to the tip of her toe

As a trainee fairy she got in a mess
When she sewed a tooth bag straight to her dress
Once she got trapped in a revolving door
She was swinging around for an hour or more

After collecting a tooth from Molly one night
She flew into the window which gave her a fright
Back in fairyland the very next day
Star's job was to empty the fairy dust tray

Not looking in front, she tripped on a case
And the fairy dust went all over her face
When they saw what had happened the others all laughed
'You're just like a clown because you're so daft'

The fairy queen said, 'I have an idea
I think I've found you a new career
You can entertain children all over town'
That's how Star became *the fairy clown.*

Molly Brimson (7)
Blackfield Junior School

The Annoying Bee

Where the water is bright and deep
A little fish lay fast asleep
Up the river and down the sea
Then he got chased by a big buzzing bee
Buzz buzz buzz and off he went
Chasing his tail like a giant serpent
He swam away as fast as he could
And then the bee stung him as hard as he could.

Ryan O'Connor (8)
Blackfield Junior School

Animal Poem

Animals are wonderful creatures,
They make lots of sounds and have amazing features,
Some have fur and some have wings
And often do some silly things.

Watching them is a beautiful sight,
But don't come near 'cause most will bite,
Seeing one wild is an absolute treasure,
Because it will give you a lot of pleasure.

Some will even go in your house,
Like the rat or the mouse
And the mite even might
Come in your house whilst you sleep at night.

Carmen Green (10)
Blackfield Junior School

Spring

In springtime
The sun will shine
And push cold winter away.

Daffodils and tulips show
That spring is on its way.

The birds sing loud
High up in the trees
To welcome in the day.

The light is brighter
The evenings lighter, and children
Can enjoy more play.

The birds and bees are willing to share
The fresh and clean spring air.

Declan Irvine (10)
Blackfield Junior School

The Knight That Knocked On My Door

The knight that knocked on my door,
He looked so very poor,
His clothes were ripped,
When he came in he tripped,
Because his feet were horribly sore.

He had a sword and a sheath
And had great big yellow teeth,
His shield was yellow,
He looked like a good fellow,
But turned out he was a thief.

He carried a bag of gold,
He looked so very bold,
His armour was metal,
He also had a petal,
I bet he was going to be sold.

The knight disappeared,
Like my worst fear
And began to run away.

Thomas Church (11)
Blackfield Junior School

My Best Friend!

I've got loads of friends at school,
Who think I'm really cool,
But there is one who I think is the best,
Funnier than all the rest.

She helps me when I'm sad,
But she can be a bit mad!
She makes me laugh all the time,
Standing in our assembly line.

She is the best as can be,
The best friend for me,
My best friend's name is . . . *Alice!*

Monica Morton (11)
Blackfield Junior School

Beneath The Sea

Their scaly skin
Glitters in the sea
When the sun shines through
The salty weeds.

A shoal of fish
Travels in time
Going backwards and forwards
Against the tide.

The clams in their shells
Clatter like teeth
On the seabed
Shimmering yellow and red.

The octopus dances
Our eight-legged friend
To the rhythm of the waves
In and out of the caves.

The elegant sea horse
Bounces up and down
It larks around
Like an underwater clown.

The life underwater
Is a magical place
As far as you can see
There's plenty of space.

Reuben Adam Capstick (8)
Blackfield Junior School

There's Something Wrong With My Family!

This is about how I live
Living with my scary sis
Sometimes I can't watch TV
My favourite programme is Newsround Showbiz
I like to eat lollies which have a fizz

I know it doesn't sound exciting
With me and my sis fighting

I have a cat who is a pig
Who loves to eat
With big strong legs
And strong feet

I have a fish called Smartie
I know it's a funny name
It's because he's multicoloured
My sister's fish aren't the same

I have a crazy family
I definitely know that
Did you know something?
There's something wrong with my cat.

Christine Hughes (8)
Blackfield Junior School

Nana

With curly white hair tucked up in bed,
Resting her sleepy head,
So old so tiny her hands so small,
My nana has never been tall.
Her eyes so blue and smiling!
She always wore her baseball hat,
She was 97 and as cool as a cat.
Her feet size one,
Has she really gone?

Sophie Bunday (10)
Blackfield Junior School

Animal!

Big brown beady eyes
And a wet black nose.
I have long ears that flap
And I hate to nap.
Can you guess who I am, yes or no?

As I run in the wind,
I am as fast as a plane.
Dodging tree after bush after tree,
Can you guess who I am yet, is that a no?
Well, shall we look and see?

My fur is golden,
But my tail is brown.
My whiskers are as long as a match,
My claws are sharp
And I love to bark,
I am a dog, you should have got that!

Charlotte Pilcher (11)
Blackfield Junior School

What A Silly Dog

My dog's name is Bugsy,
His coat's all soft and snugsy,
He spins round and round,
Until he falls on the ground.

He fell in the pond
And had a bad response,
He came out all wet,
What a silly silly pet.

When he sees his lead,
He runs and jumps with speed,
He barks like mad,
If he doesn't get a walk, he's sad.

That's my dog Bugsy.

Zoe Hanley (11)
Blackfield Junior School

Thunder

As the thunder roared,
I clutched up tight,
And the rain came down,
But that was light!

Boom! says the thunder,
I jumped with fright
And weed myself,
In the middle of the night!

'Mum, Mum!'
I cried using might,
'Don't worry my dear,
We're all right.'

Clatter, crash, boom, bang!
The house fell down,
So my ears rang.

I'm writing this,
From a hospital bed,
Not bad actually,
Since I have a bad head!

Marie Atkinson (10)
Blackfield Junior School

Dolphins

Slipping, sliding through the sea,
As I have always done throughout history,
Swimming by boats as they row
And eating fish as I go.
Jumping through hoops in a display,
The crowd all cheer, *hip hip hooray!*
Clicking noises as we speak
Can be heard even when the weather's bleak
We live a long time, growing old
Who knows what the future may hold.

Charlotte Willbourne (10)
Blackfield Junior School

Creature

With its dark green back and red breast
You have to call it lovely at least
Its coat shines as it flies west
This is no beast

Its head turns and stays motionless in the air
It concentrates on the water
Waiting for a fish to leave its lair
Rarely does it falter

With a sudden dive it drops in mid-air
Its prey is about to lose its life
It doesn't care
It points its beak-knife

It hits the water with a splash
Down it does go
It disappears in a flash
What happens here I don't know

Seconds later it rises again
A fish in its bill
It goes to a branch, then
It's ready for a meal.

Mark Stevens (10)
Blackfield Junior School

Our Sky

Our sky is big,
Our sky is bright,
Our sky is very dark at night.

Our sky is clear,
Our sky is blue,
Our sky makes our holidays come true.

Our sky is bare,
Our sky is there,
Our sky is everywhere.

Laura Vincent (8)
Blackfield Junior School

Holidays

I can't wait till my holiday comes,
I'm counting on my fingers and thumbs.
I can't wait to jump in the pool,
My holiday will be really cool.

Now the day has finally arrived,
Up on the plane I will fly.
To my destination I will go,
Hip hip hooray, I'll soon arrive.

Finally I'm here,
I will have lots of fun,
Building sandcastles in the sun
And splashing in the swimming pool.

Oh no! My holiday's at an end
So quickly over, surely not
But it is
I'll have to wait until next year.

Matthew Amess (10)
Blackfield Junior School

Spring To Life

After a cold winter,
Which I struggled to survive,
All of the trees are waiting,
For the celebration to begin.

I add all of my beautiful buds
And my fresh spring perfume.
Looking at myself in the glinting water's reflection,
Absolutely beautiful!

As the town clock strikes midnight,
All of the trees huddle together,
Having an amazing time,
Partying till dawn.

Daryl Price (11)
Blackfield Junior School

If I had A Cloud's Pocket

If I had a cloud's pocket,
There'd be bright blue skies
And the deep dark nights.

If I had a cloud's pocket,
There'd be the bright yellow sun
And a shining silver moon with its wishing stars.

If I had a cloud's pocket,
There'd be showers of rain
And blowing wind rustling the leaves.

If I had a cloud's pocket,
I'd keep the rockets from the moon
And the men that go up.

If I had a cloud's pocket,
I'd capture birds that fly by
And aeroplanes that zoom past.

But if I didn't have my pocket,
Where would they be?
I would lay on the ground and watch them above.

Emma Tregarthen (9)
Blackfield Junior School

Strike!

Slowly creeping, watching my prey,
Hidden in the long grass, no more
Than four feet away, ready to strike,
But what is this, a flash of orange
The other side of the herd!
I had to be quick. Curse that stupid tiger!
He needs to be taught a lesson.

Later that night, creeping to the young
Tiger's lair, I struck with a mighty
Slash, killing instantly!

Shaun Rollinson (10)
Blackfield Junior School

The Train Ride

Faster than Concorde
Faster than a plane
Lorries filling up with grain.

People dashing everywhere
Young children stop and stare.

Boats are honking loud and clear
People chanting can you hear?

Fast food is smelling great
Hurry up don't be late.

Preparing for another adventure
Through the countryside
Hooray! Hooray Hooray! Hooray!

Emma Brown (10)
Blackfield Junior School

My Two Cats

My two cats always fight,
They even fight at night,
They have big green eyes
And love catching flies.

My cats love to eat
And love little treats,
They come for rubs to me
And paw me when I have my tea.

I really really love my cats,
Even though they can be brats,
I look out for my cats all the time
And they will always be mine.

Grant Adlem (10)
Blackfield Junior School

The Young Penguin

It's warm in here
But it's time to get out
I peck against the hard shell with all my might
I'm free and what can I see?
I feel and it is so cold!

I look around and what a sight
I look up and what a height
My father looks proud
He has me firm against his tummy
And I can't move around.

I'm so ugly and fluffy
He is so beautiful, black and white with gold
I want to be like him, so stunning and bold
He waddles when he walks, but that's no shame
Because all the others are doing the same.

The noise is deafening
The shrill squawks and the slip slap walks
Diving into the ice-cold waters
Flying under the blue icebergs
Filling their stomachs with fish - I've heard!

The sun has gone down, the sky is black
The southern lights fill up the night
I'm safe and warm, here with my dad
Huddle together one and all
To be an emperor penguin - I'm so glad.

Joshua Capstick (10)
Blackfield Junior School

The Osprey

Flying high, flying free,
Osprey on the wind you ride;
Flying high, flying free,
Spread your wings so far and wide.

In the land of heather and highlands,
The osprey flies over the moors.
Scanning the hills for danger,
As with speed he dives and soars.

In the land of cliffs and canyons,
The egg collectors lurk,
Killing off those osprey chicks -
That's their dirty work.

Do not steal those osprey chicks
They don't belong to you.
You've no right to take their lives
And threaten freedom too.

Swooping down to catch its prey,
As safe and silent as an arrow from a bow.
Its daily meal for the day
Will be hit with such a force, he'll never know.

Sasha Hutton (11)
Blackfield Junior School

Cats!

Fluffy furry ball of fluff,
Tearing, chewing quite rough,
Sleeping eyes shut make no sound,
Purring, twitching running around,
Playing in the garden with his friends,
Wishing the day would never end,
Curling up on my lap,
Now he's ready for his nap!

Holly Kinggett (10)
Blackfield Junior School

Sunset Castle

Everything is quiet
The saffron sun's rays reach out
To touch the ragged rocks
As the sun slips away
The rippling waves
Are sad to see it go.

The multi-coloured sky
Vividly rests in the gentle breeze
Cradling the water and the sun
The forgotten castle
Is proud and the ruins
Stand strong

The hills are neatly packed away
With emerald-green grass swaying
The elevated rocks stand tall and firm
Waving away the placid sun
And beautiful sky.

Aimee Paddick (10)
Calmore Junior School

Rain

Splashing rain pours,
Rippling in puddles,
Dropping in drains,
Jumping in puddles.

Rain forming,
Into beasts,
Dropping away,
To fight another day.

Daniel Cornick (10)
Calmore Junior School

Rain

The rain,
shooting down bangs on the roof
lands on a car but no dent
off into a puddle.
Suddenly the puddle runs like
little men running down a street.
But then it dries up like dark demons
being shot with arrows of light.

As the dark kingdom runs away
to fight another day,
a colourful bridge forms
to welcome
the knight of light,
but as he comes
over the bridge,
the demons
fire their balls of darkness,
to conquer the knight
and as mysteriously as he
came he disappears
to fight another day!

Philip Hemborough (10)
Calmore Junior School

In The Woods

The rustling of the trees as they sway in the wind
And the sounds of howling far in the distance,
With a cold breeze running through my hair.
I am lost, far from my home.
It's getting cold and dark.
When the creatures of the night awake,
I am sad and scared.

Megan Philpott (9)
Calmore Junior School

Naughty Little Raindrop

The naughty little raindrop,
Decided to run away,
So he packed his tiny suitcase
And decided to say goodbye.

It rained and it rained,
He was blown everywhere,
The naughty little raindrop
Landed on a car.

The car stopped
At a wonderful beach,
He took all his things
And jumped.

He ambled a while,
He walked and walked,
Took a dive right into the sea
And he was soaked by the sea back home.

A little while later,
It rains once again,
This time he lands,
On a school building.

Oh no! the little raindrop,
Down the gutter he is going,
He's made a friend,
What an adventure!

Rachel Healy (9)
Calmore Junior School

Sunset

The bright yellow sunset
Reached out like grabbing hands
To touch the old strong castle rocks.
The castle still stands
As the castle is sad to see it die.

Kieran Whittle (9)
Calmore Junior School

Hearing Fish Wriggling Slowly

Hearing fish wriggling slowly
Hearing water splashing about
Hearing children rampaging around
Hearing teachers chattering on

Seeing chairs dark and brown
Seeing classrooms big and bold
Seeing lights bright as bright as can be
Seeing clocks ticking slowly

Smelling carpet, it is dusty and old
Smelling water it is wrinkled and clear

Touching my pen, smooth and hard
Touching a table, wooden and bright.

Brandon May (11)
Calmore Junior School

The Weather

Sun shining down on me,
Trees waving can't you see,
Now comes drips of rain,
Banging on my windowpane.

Rainbow twinkling up above,
Flying around it is a dove,
Fading slowly away it goes,
When will it come back no one knows.

Wind whistling side to side,
Whizzing round like a ride,
Twirling and swirling right behind,
I wonder what else we will find.

Emma Bundy (9)
Calmore Junior School

The Stormy Night!

The trees are a beast,
Trying to eat the houses like a roaring lion.
The wind is howling angrily,
Like wolves searching for their prey.

The cars are policemen;
Keeping crime out of the neighbourhood;
Watching careful like a police camera.
The rain is heavy rocks,
Making disaster everywhere it falls.

The neighbourhood is crying out for help,
Like several babies locked up in a shed;
Until the storm suddenly pauses
And the storm is brought to an end.

The grass is rustling quietly,
Like a mouse on an adventure.
The wind is whistling quietly
Like a jolly milkman.
The night is dawning but the sun is rising
For a brand new day!

Gemma Sowamber (10)
Calmore Junior School

Everywhere

Seeing the blackboard as it magically writes on words,
Seeing the shoes walking trying to get to a nice warm classroom,
Seeing the pen write words and then its nib breaks in half,
Seeing the paper drift high above the clouds and then back down,
Seeing the door swing open then shut . . .

Hearing the children's feet thudding loudly against the floor,
Hearing the wind whispering, trying to tell me something,
Hearing the sound of pencils' leads breaking,
Hearing people trying to talk through the shouting,
Hearing the chairs trying to move to the nearest exit . . .

Zoe Swash (10)
Calmore Junior School

Nature Of My School

I hear the birds chirping in their nest,
I hear the other kids shouting at their best,
I hear singing as the wind blows softly,
I hear the angry teachers telling children to be good,
I hear people screaming like a hurricane . . .

I see the tree leaves sparkling in the light,
I see doors opening and closing as the wind strikes them,
I see the grass swaying like clouds moving,
I see chairs with a rough surface that looks like a stony floor,
I see tables with books stacked in piles built like a tower,
I see the whiteboard glisten in the morning light . . .

I smell the sizzling pizza as I line up for lunch,
I smell the air as it rushes past my face,
I smell orange from a kid's lunch which he had enjoyed eating,
I smell pineapple as I search for my lunchbox . . .

As I gently touch my pen I think of games,
As I touch my reading book I felt I was flying,
The touch of my pencil makes me shoot in mid-air,
The touch of my trousers, make me think of my brother . . .

I taste the sweet juice pouring out of my apple like a rushing waterfall,
I taste the strong flavour of salt and vinegar crisps,
I taste crackers with cheese spread on top . . .

Amy Gasser (11)
Calmore Junior School

Hurricane!

Hurricane hurricane go away
Dark cloud, rain all coming at once
Pitter-patter pitter-patter the rain taps on my roof.
Whoosh whoosh the wind goes by.
Crash crash the cars hit together.
Crack crack the windows crack.

Stefan Scott (9)
Calmore Junior School

School Senses

Watching Mrs Swainston working in the office,
Watching children run down the corridor,
Watching the fish swim aimlessly around their tank,
Watching helpers roam through the school,
Watching the door as still as a dead body.

Listening to the fridge's music,
Listening to musicians and their instruments,
Listening to the chattering children.

Touching the steel pan's cold, shiny surface,
Touching the bed's fluffy blanket in the medical room.

Smelling the fresh air as you step out into the cold,
I watch the building get smaller and smaller as I walk slowly home
At three o'clock.

Alice Morris (10)
Calmore Junior School

Fish Friends

Hearing bubbles burst as they reach the surface of the tank
Hearing the faraway talking of other children and teachers
Hearing footsteps coming closer . . . closer . . . closer

Seeing fish swim round like satellites in space
Seeing fish and catfish frightened and not knowing where to go
Seeing sea snails stick to the tank as if trying to get out

Smelling the strange odour of uneaten fish food
Smelling the stale air as we open the lid.

Louanne Jones (10)
Calmore Junior School

The Big Bang

The
The big
The big bang
The big bang boom!
Two asteroids huge
Two asteroids massive
Great Titans, in the universe endless
Great Titans, in the heavens high
In the universe, endless
In the heavens, empty
They collide with a sickening crunch!
They collide with a nauseating, earth-shattering crunch!
Out of the explosion, planets were made
Out of the explosion, planet, creation.

Peter Bone (11)
Calmore Junior School

My Creation

He came to bring love and light
He came to bring peace all around
He came to rock me, he came to cradle me away
When he first stepped
When he first stepped in
The world was round
The world was round and small
He made it grow
He made it grow with happiness
Then he rained
Then he rained and made a flood
He was so upset
He was so upset and filled the sky with colour.

Ashleigh Murray (10)
Calmore Junior School

Who Made Our Earth?

His Earth wasn't big
His Earth wasn't big at all
He laid in the sun to heat up
He laid in the rain to cool down
His Earth was nice
His Earth was nice to lay on
He looked at his Earth
He looked at his Earth from a rock
He spoke like a woman
He spoke like a young woman
He loved his Earth
He loved his little Earth
He blew the wind
He blew the cold wind
He sprung from an egg
He sprung from a little egg
He made everything
He made trees and rocks.

Michael King (10)
Calmore Junior School

My School Senses

Hearing the sound of a whistle blow as loud as an elephant's trunk
Hearing teachers talking
Hearing the footsteps, the laughing, the shouting
Hearing the sweet music

The feel of the cold wood on my fingertips
The rough surface of the wallpaper scratches my arm as I walk by

Smelling the fresh air
Smelling the fish food as the fish get fed

Seeing the world hung above me
Seeing a dreamcatcher catching my dreams

This is my world.

Zoe Shore (11)
Calmore Junior School

The World Created By An Alien!

Once there was an alien
Once there was an alien called *Zibzab!*
He used his magic power
He used his magic power called bull strength
'I'm wicked I'm cool'
'I'm magic I rule!'
'I'll come down to Earth and create humans and stuff'
'Humans that speak like us us us'

For days he worked
For days he worked to create this crazy planet.
On the fifteenth day he looked around
On the fifteenth day he looked around at what he'd made,
He was ashamed.
He was ashamed at the manners and respect of the people.

He left it
He left it for good
'They can finish it off themselves themselves themselves.'

Ian Chilcott (10)
Calmore Junior School

The Library

Seeing the books glimmer on the shelf
Seeing a chair stuck in the corner
Seeing the people reading with their noses in the book

Smelling the delicious smell of food in people's lunchboxes
Smelling the new carpet

Hearing loud chattering all around me
Hearing pages of books flipping

Touching the soft, slippery covers of the books
Touching the chair's rough surface, like sand
Touching the shiny and rough wall.

James Whitcher (10)
Calmore Junior School

Winter

S now is fun!
N ow is the time to play in the snow!
O ranges are in your stockings
W ow you've got a pencil case

I t is Christmas Eve!
S tockings are fun to open

F reddy is fun to play with
A nna can do a jigsaw puzzle
L ook Lilly
L illy I have a lollipop!
I 'm going to bed
N o I have not
G irls are good!

Anna Brown (8)
Harrison Primary School

Snow Poem

Soft as lambswool
Cold as frozen bread
Wet as an adult duck
Pretty as a crystal
Light as a feather
Snow!
Fairies are sprinkling snow
Like a long thick blanket
They blow on the lake
And make crystal ice
The children are surprised to see the snow
They get their things and go
But they do not know whose fingers
Have made the snow.

Hannah Luckett (7)
Harrison Primary School

Snowman

S now glittering all round the garden
N oise of a crackly icicle
O ver the whole field lies white snow like a cloud park
W hite like a cloudy blanket
M ighty ice statues
A shimmery white carpet
N umb noses and fingers, stiff with the cold.

Charlie Thorpe (7)
Harrison Primary School

Snow

Like a velvet blanket waiting for me to snuggle up in,
It's like a winter wonderland,
Branches are dazzling with icicles,
Branches shimmering with snow,
Reindeers clip-clopping around,
Children playing in the snow,
A snow queen riding through the trees,
Snowflakes glittering on the ground,
I can see spiky holly trees.

Maddie Penny (7)
Harrison Primary School

Panda

It seems forever we've been here
Only you can end our fear

The world around me is so dark
The hunting dogs begin to bark

We're all being hunted
Our race has nearly ended.

Aiden Bryant (10)
Newbridge Junior School

The Fox!

I'm fast
I'm sly
I'll zoom past
I like to be a spy

I have thick fur
Everyone must desire
Catching my prey is sometimes a blur
I'm so clever don't you see

I lick my lips
I grind my teeth
Chasing my dinner I never miss
I smell the rabbits from the dirt beneath

I'm fast
I'm sly
I'd zoom past
I like to be a spy.

Christopher Sculthorp (10)
Newbridge Junior School

Guess My Name

Eating, eating they are so delicious.
Green, green they dazzle my eyes,
They persuade me with all their might.

My ears point up like bats asleep,
I mean no harm to any animal,
I have a bendy, stick neck.

My friends call me giraffe.
Giraffe, giraffe, giraffe.
That is what they call me!

My ears point up like bats asleep,
I mean no harm to any animal,
I have a bendy stick neck.

Thomas Arnfeld (9)
Newbridge Junior School

Rainbow!

I'm red, I'm blue, I'm purple and green
I'm all different colours . . . I'll never be seen
I'm polkadotted, stripy, the same colour as you
I sit by the river so I can turn blue

I'm always like a rainbow
I'm a different colour each day
I'm a chameleon
Hip hip hooray

I like to be a chameleon
No one can see me
I like to use camouflage
No one can be me

I'm always like a rainbow
I'm a different colour each day
I'm a chameleon
Hip hip hooray.

Lauren Hammond (9)
Newbridge Junior School

Guess Who?

The darkness swept over my fierce blue eyes
I smelt the smell of meat nearby
I went to pounce but I heard a ripple
It must be tricking me I'm near the water
I heard some footsteps so I put my paw forward
Oh no I can feel my black stripes getting wetter

I'm under the water it's the end for me
I can see the fish in the water
I tried to swim but it was no use
I can see something in the water it's bigger than me
I'm dying I'm dying I only wanted some dinner
Help it's trying to eat me
I'm dying I'm dying I'm dead.

Gemma Gatward (10)
Newbridge Junior School

I Am A Golden Eagle

I am as large as a Condor,
A beak as sharp as a knife.
You sneak up on your prey
And it loses its life.

I swoop down from my nest,
I pick out a feast,
My fur is as soft as a hare,
I am such a beast.

I'm like a dart,
It is freezing cold.
I'm not like him,
He's very bold.

I am as fast as a train,
I'm like a machine gun.
Now I'm not cold,
I'm as hot as the sun.

I'm really hungry,
I need some meat.
Do you know how I catch my prey?
I use my feet.

I'm nearly extinct,
I'm really red.
I am now frozen
And I'm dead.

Kieran Farrugia (9)
Newbridge Junior School

Black Widow Spider

So black, tiny and poisonous
Small, scary
Slow, steady
Black widow spider

A femme fatale
One gender
Female!
After mating
Males die
Black widow spider

Slow when moving
Poisons quick
You'd better watch out
Or else!
Ouch!
Black widow spider

A femme fatale
One gender
Female!
After mating
Males die
Black widow spider.

Sophie Lee (10)
Newbridge Junior School

What Am I?

He walks through the jungle,
As quiet as can be,
The stripy predator,
Is hunting for his tea.

Hunting low,
Hunting high,
Is that my next meal
In the sky?

I see something,
In front of me,
It looks delicious, it looks divine,
It looks like I am just in time.

It's ran away,
That wretched beast,
I wish my hunger,
Would just cease.

Here comes the hunters,
It's time for me to hide,
I find a hut,
I creep inside.

I can't be heard,
I can't be seen,
Or they'll kill me,
Aren't they mean.

Rhiannon Smithard (10)
Newbridge Junior School

Pouncing Tiger

My fur is striped,
I see my prey,
I want it not to run away.

My white paws patting on the ground,
As I hear, I make no sound,
My eyes are glinting from the sun,
I catch my prey and then it's done.

My teeth are jagged,
Rough and white,
I creep around in the night.

I get to pounce upon my prey,
I live on for another day!

Katie Heap (10)
Newbridge Junior School

Gorilla

As fury as silk
As black as no lights
Don't go too close
Or he'll give you a fright

Here come the huntsman
The gorillas look worried
If you shoot a gorilla
That's when you'll be sorry

They live in the jungle
So fragile and green
Watch out, look out
That's when they get mean.

Sam Eaton (10)
Newbridge Junior School

The Monkey's Song

I'm twirling, whirling in the trees,
Even though people try to kill me,
Jump and jump and glide in the air,
Men cut down my home and it's not fair.

I'm orange and small.
And I'm not very tall,
My feet go patter,
But to you it doesn't matter.

My kind is dying,
We are no longer flying,
So stop killing me,
So I can live peacefully.

This is my song,
The world is so wrong,
This is my plea,
So I can be free.

Ruby Helms (10)
Newbridge Junior School

Whale In The Sea

In the blue swaying sea,
I am swimming along trying to make it home safely,
There are piranhas swimming around,
Why do you want me?
I'm only used for my blubber,
I can see torture and killing,
Splish, splash, splosh, here come the knives,
I am stabbed,
All I can feel are the knives in my stomach.

I am crying, dying,
Nobody cares,
I'm on the bottom of the sea *dead.*

Samantha Chearman (10)
Newbridge Junior School

Who Am I . . . ?

The beady eyes, the long thin tail,
Nothing to keep me in my jail.
I run around and squeeze through bars,
I hide under bushes they make my home.

I go to my nest for wintertime,
The temperature drops below freezing,
I am asleep within seconds.

The beady eyes the long thin tail,
Nothing to keep me in my jail.
I run around and squeeze through bars,
I hide under bushes they make my home.

When I wake up, I smell the sweet air,
A new year dawns, and I have not a care.

The beady eyes the long thin tail,
Nothing to keep me in my jail.
I run around and squeeze through bars,
I hide under bushes they make my home.

Madeline Goodchild (10)
Newbridge Junior School

Guess My Animal?

I have black stripes.
I also have orange skin as charming as a sun.
My skin is thick as leather.
I'm hunting for my food.

I have teeth as sharp as sharks.
I'm running as fast as I can.
Trying to find meat.
I'm hunting for my food.

I'm starving.
I haven't had my dinner when I was little.
I don't have a family now.
My family left me when I was very little.

Katie Lee (10)
Newbridge Junior School

The Chase

Blood rushing round and round
I hear footsteps rocking against the pebbles
Dark shadows running
I smell sewage from the river
My sore feet are slapping against the pebbles
Brushing past people as I sprint

I feel like a deer running from a hunter
Oh no! I've come to a gate, I quickly climb over
My palms are all sweaty
I can hear birds shouting 'Pick pocket, pick pocket' in my head
Hurry hurry! Yes I've lost them!
My head is spinning

What a relief
Now I can calm down
My heart is slowing down
My legs are aching
I need to sit down
Now I'll have to watch my back.

Natalie Rose (10)
Newbridge Junior School

The Seeking Cobra

Seeking through the jungle
Slithering across the floor,
Looking for delicious prey
My tummy's rumbling badly.

Almost got the prey nearly
There's a distant rumble from afar,
Oh no it must be thunder
As the rain comes the prey runs away.

Trooping home without any food
I slide quickly up to the top of the tree,
I'm lucky to have a home away from the rain
I'm especially lucky to be a cobra.

Sharna Johnson (10)
Newbridge Junior School

They're Behind Me

They have seen,
They're coming, they're coming.
I know where they're going,
Forward, around the corner,
Past Hatton Garden,
To Chart Street,
Drip, drip, sweat on my forehead,
Pigeons scatter,
Footsteps bang down behind me,
I can hear my heart,
Thump, thump, thump,
I hide in a doorway,
They have lost me,
I come out - they see me,
I turn the corner,
Dismal shadows in front,
I jump back,
My face turning red,
I start running,
My sweating hands touch my neck,
The noose isn't there,
An owl hoots,
I stop to rest,
I can't hear footsteps,
They've stopped,
They've stopped,
My heart is slowing down, down, down,
I did it, I made it, I'm safe,
A smile of glee on face,
- Until next time.

Bracken Pluckrose (10)
Newbridge Junior School

Free

The patter of my tiny feet
Against the marshy floor,
My small brown prickly ears
Listening out for danger,
My tiny beady eyes
Looking for food,
Splashing in the water
Catching scaly fish,
The ripples of the water
And the whip of my tail,
Nothing to keep me locked up
Not a single rail.

Diving, diving down for a catch
Trying to mind the rapids,
One day I know I'll die
But I might as well live my life,
And continue my family's life
The ripples on the water,
And the whip of my tail
Noting to keep me locked up,
Not a single rail.

Bethany Goodchild (10)
Newbridge Junior School

Spider Verse

Make my web nice and neat
Lots of black flies good to eat
I'm quite small eight legs too
I'll eat my dinner in front of you
You eat us when you're asleep
Five or six times, we crawl up your feet
Lots of different types of spider
The spider is an excellent glider
Black widow tarantulas too
All those types are meant to scare you!

Rosie Robertson (10)
Newbridge Junior School

Colourful Chameleon

I'm red, I'm green
I'm blue, I'm pink.
I'm more . . .
Colourful than you
Red, pink, orange, purple
Yellow, peach, blue
Colourful than you.

I can turn red
I can turn green
I can turn pink
I can turn orange
I can turn purple
I can turn yellow
I can turn peach
I can turn blue
C . . . c . . . c . . . c . . . colours.

Stripes, stripes
Making me dizzy
Spots, spots
Getting all jazzed.
C . . . c . . . c . . . c . . . colours
Red, pink, orange, purple,
Yellow, peach, blue.

'Help me, help me' I can't fall to sleep
My amazing day cannot stop now
I'm a chameleon, I should stay up late
I'm made of colours, c . . . c . . . c . . . c . . . colours
I'm red, I'm blue, more colourful than you.

Amber Jane Privett (9)
Newbridge Junior School

Joey

I am a baby,
I'm so tough,
But sometimes,
I get too rough.

I sit in my mum's
Warm pouch,
It's just like
A comfy couch.

I've got soft fur,
I must admit,
But sometimes
Animals bite it.

I've got pointy ears,
They're a lovely brown,
People stroke me but
Hunt me down.

Oh no, I'd better run,
A hunter I can see,
Oh no, I'd better run,
Oh help, he caught me.

I think I'm going to cry,
Here's my last goodbye,
I wonder if my mum knows,
I'm about to die.

Lauren Dewhurst (9)
Newbridge Junior School

The Chase

Darting through alleyways,
My ribs hurting,
Men gaining,
Why did I go there?

Garbage stinking,
Rats squeaking,
Men gaining,
Why did I go there?

Voices shouting,
Cobbles rocking,
Men gaining,
Why did I go there?

I took a wrong turn,
Is this the end?
Men gaining,
Why did I go there?

I jump a wall,
Never should have done it,
I lost them,
And ran back home,
Why did I go there?

Daniel Belstone (11)
Newbridge Junior School

The Jaguar

Hunting, seeking through the jungle,
Teeth like knives, blood all over them,
Waiting to pounce on its delicious prey,
Feared by all the smaller animals,
Oh no, it's running away.

I nearly caught it,
You can hear it squeaking as I am running up behind it,
Starving to death,
Feared by all the smaller animals,
Need to find more food.

Trekking through the jungle,
No food or drink around,
Crack goes a branch as it falls off a tree,
Disturbing my prey,
Feared by all the smaller animals,
As it runs away.

As I run after my prey,
I dig my teeth into a mouse,
It tastes absolutely delicious.

Georgina Anne Nicholls (10)
Newbridge Junior School

Man Hunt

Sweat dribbling down my head,
Dark alleys up ahead,
Smelly pavement, is a stench,
Legs are weakening, need a bench,
Coming to a dead end,
Myself I cannot defend,
My blood is now quickening its pace,
Look everywhere just in case,
I'll end up on a hangman's rope,
This I cannot cope,
Fingers are trembling,
Looking at the document,
Got to run faster,
My brain is bent,
Rats are crawling up my legs,
Spine is tingling,
Oh! I'm blind!
Coming nearer from behind,
Darkness, black, coal running down my eyes,
Bent over need a rest,
Running, running, doing my best.

Harvey Scott-Cooper (10)
Newbridge Junior School

Horses' Life

As we canter aside each other,
Darting through the trees,
We look behind sharply and see a *hunter,*
We go our separate ways.

Hair flying through the fresh calm air,
Galloping faster and faster through the grass,
Trying to get away but *bang!* you're dead,
The sound of hooves clapping on the grass floor.

With the last ounce of breath you yell,
That is it eternal life,
The echo of your yell rings through my head,
You're gone but not for long,
He gets me too . . . *bang!*

Now I am with you forever,
We're gone together.
Stuck in a paradise field.

Yasmin Wells (10)
Newbridge Junior School

The Panther

I hear the sound of the pitter-patter of my feet
Like the dripping of a tap.
I see the blurry forest trees as I sprint by,
I feel the fur of my cubs, as they run past me,
I smell the scent of rotting leaves.
My black fur being rushed back in the wind.

I taste dry air, as I speed to my trees,
There's a click and then a bang.
It must be the gunshots from the hunter's revolver.
I climb my tree as I try not to slip.
I rest on a branch as I watch my cubs run.
Soon the day is over, I'm sinking into the darkness.

Toby Walton (9)
Newbridge Junior School

Run Away

Tap, tap, tap,
I hear them coming up behind me,
Gliding across the gleaming cobbles,
My heart beats rapidly like a lion,
My tongue pants like a dog.

I slip sneakily around the corner
And down the alley I bolt.
I scuttle, I scamper,
Become a shadow.

An excruciating pain digs into my side, like a rusty sword,
Disappear, reappear,
Disappear, reappear,
Disappear, reappear,
Disappear, reappear,
Disappear.

Are they all still there?
Gone!

Jackson Ball (11)
Newbridge Junior School

The Clever Monkey

He stumbles through the forest,
Swaying through the breeze,
Sniffing and snuffling,
Now his mind is at ease.

Along came a fly,
He passed the monkey by,
Then he gave a sigh
And started to cry.

And then he stopped
Because his tummy popped.
He started to hop
And then just then flopped.

Joseph Quinlan (9)
Newbridge Junior School

The Chase

Men in brown are chasing me
Time is ticking
Heart is thumping
Coughing and spluttering
As I run
Men in brown are chasing me
Feet are aching
Hands are sweaty
Legs are weak
As I run
Men in brown are chasing me
Head is hot
Pigeons squeaking
Pulse is picking up
As I run
Men in brown are chasing me
Shadows black
It's getting cold
It's getting darker
As I run
I hope the document's still there!

Emily Tann (11)
Newbridge Junior School

They're Coming

They're coming
They're coming
They're coming for me
Down roads
Round alleys
Hiding among the trees
I hear their footsteps
I hear their footsteps
I crouch in the corner, stiff as ice
There's a deafening silence
I close my eyes
I know I'm not safe
I run
Down roads
Round alleys
Hiding among the trees
I'm safe
I'm safe
I walk away
I smile
I smile
Till another day.

Ashleigh Muns (11)
Newbridge Junior School

The Chase

I'm sprinting, sweating
Running out of breath
Feeling walls, smelling sweat
Running riot
Glancing back
Seeing walls and fences
Hearing cries
Dodging people
Crowded with eyes
As people are pushed over aggressively
By the chasers of myself
I'm holding on
To the document
My pulse rate quickening
My heart is pumping harder
Racing rapidly
Through the great dark streets
Can I keep up this pace?
I'm looking back
But cannot see
Who is really chasing me.

Andrew Bentley (10)
Newbridge Junior School

That's So Unfair

That's so unfair,
I live here, not him
Anyway he's so scruffy
He drinks,
You can smell it on his breath,
It stinks.
He looks like a pick pocket,
A pipe,
What's he doing?
Does he know it's bad for him?
He probably thinks,
Because my dad's vulnerable and blind,
He can come into this house and steal,
He thinks wrong.
I'll be watching him like a hawk,
He won't get anywhere with my eyes on him!

Claire Norman (11)
Newbridge Junior School

The Chase

Men are following in the street,
I can hear the footsteps as they beat.
Got to get to a safe place,
I can imagine the anger on their face.
Trying to catch my breath real quick,
I'm gong to be beaten with a stick.

I can hear their voices in the air,
I'll never know if they'll be there.
Will I get found or will I not?
The clothes on me start to rot.
Houses flash by as I run,
They won't stop until they're done!

Shane Filleul (11)
Newbridge Junior School

The Chase

I feel scared, frightened,
I'm running with buildings towering over me,
With the bright stars shining in my eyes,
I see shadows on the left side of me,
The men's footsteps slowly fading away,
I feel the cold cobbled stones on my bare feet.

Dodging in and out of quiet streets,
As I hear the hoot of an owl,
The pick pocketing has led me into grave danger,
My sweating hands trembling as I feel in my pocket for the scroll,
In my mind I hear the pigeons squawking pick pocket, pick pocket,
                                                    over and over,
Running through the same streets again and again.

I'm running as fast as a cheetah stumbling as I do,
More owls hooting,
When suddenly the footsteps stop,
At last I've lost them,
It's over at last,
It's over at last,
It's over at last.

Kim Allison (11)
Newbridge Junior School

The Chase

The wind is rushing ahead,
Getting colder each second,
My teeth are chattering, my bones are bashing,
With coldness.

Whatever shall I do?
I'm hoping they're not near.
I'm rushing, I'm rushing, I'm running, I'm running,
With fear.

My heartbeat is beating faster every second,
My shadow is moving slower,
I'm coming to a dead end,
Help, help, what do I do?
Should I turn and run their way?
Should I climb the wall,
Or should I drop and let them get me?

My brain is full with questions,
Are they near?
Are they far?
All I know, is that they won't give up.

Harriet Standen (10)
Newbridge Junior School

The Chase

I run rapidly,
Thump, thump, thump goes my heart,
Sharp pains grip my sides,
Blood pumping around my body fast,
I look round quickly to see if they are following me,
My cheeks are red, I can feel it,
I feel like I'm a wolf or a fox being hunted down,
My hearing is very good, their hurrying footsteps beat louder
With every stride as they attempt to catch me,
I turn round the corner quick,
I hear them say 'where's he gone?'
I can hear the birds saying 'pick pocket pick pocket' in my head,
I stop,
I peek round the corner,
They've gone,
I feel relieved,
My heart slows down,
I take deep breaths as my chest tightens
With every passing second of the chase,
Suddenly I get a splitting headache,
I go back to the Red Lion Tavern,
They are there, they were waiting for me,
Help me, help me,
I run as fast as I can,
They start chasing me,
I look round,
They aren't there,
I've lost them,
Finally I'm safe,
But for how long?
This question is running through my mind and it won't stop.

Chelsea Kellett (10)
Newbridge Junior School

The Chase

I had taken some paper
Two men had killed that man
Stab! Thump! Scream!
I pushed myself against the wall.

I slipped away they heard
They had seen me
I had to run
They were following me.

I was dodging the moonlight
I glanced back speedily
I had a stitch in my chest
I jumped over a family of rats.

I was sweating
I wasn't going to stop
Their footsteps were like hooves
Their footsteps were gradually dying away.

I thought I had lost them
They jumped out at me
Were they ever going to stop?
What have I gotten myself into?

My sisters had always told me
Keep away from strange people
Why had I picked his pocket?
Should I drop it, and let them have it?

I had lost them
I was safe at last.

Jake Lawrence (10)
Newbridge Junior School

The Chase

Running away along the cobbled streets,
I can hear them coming.
Darting here, hiding there,
The great houses towering above me.

I'm back in front of them,
I can see them coming,
They're getting closer,
My breathing is getting heavy.

I run along Cot's Court,
I can smell them coming.
My pulse is quickening,
I run rapidly down an alleyway.

I am scared almost frightened of them,
I can hear their breath,
What are my sisters going to say?
I wish I'd never taken that piece of paper.

Suddenly I can't see them anymore,
I sprint silently around to check they're not there.
They're not there,
They've gone!

Katie-May Firth (10)
Newbridge Junior School

The Chase

In the shadows I dart about,
Round corners, alleys and roads,
Closer, closer, closer they get,
Blood rushes to my head,
Aching feet on the cold cobbles,
The man in brown, will catch me,
I take a breath,
I hide in the dark,
The moonlight has found me
And so have they,
Off I go again,
Round corners, alleys and roads,
The murmuring of my sisters' voices
Are shouting in my head,
I can feel them breathing down my neck,
They're getting closer,
My legs are in pain,
Can't stop now!
Won't stop now!
I can,
They've gone,
A sigh of relief!
Gasping for air,
I hide.

Cally Surman (11)
Newbridge Junior School

The Chase

The scary shadows, the fast pace,
My blood rushing as I dodge.
Coughing, coughing, as I lean onto a wall,
I wait, then look, and I carry on.

I turn the corner, crack there was a wall,
I can hear their footsteps along the cobbled ground.
My cheeks are flushed,
My heart is bursting, my head is spinning, I'm scared.

It's dark,
Birds are screeching, their wings are flapping,
My sisters' voices, 'Oh Smith what have you got yourself into?'
The men have gone.

I think they have gone back to The Lion Tavern,
I'm sweating.

Natalie King (11)
Newbridge Junior School

The Day God Released Me!

White in front, fear behind,
I can't go back not now I'm here,
Rushing pictures in my head,
No one else to comfort me,
Revenge I hear scared and lonely,
Smoke, black and thick, wants me to see it,
I have been touched by God good or bad,
But I smell hatred,
What now,
I turn all I see is black,
Slowly it opens, I'm released
It's gone, it's disappeared,
Rescue me!

Bethany Meredith (11)
North Baddesley Junior School

Senses

Dust flying up from the ground,
As the shaking foot touches it,
A slam of the foot shatters up his leg,
The trees rushing past as the boy is running so fast,
From Queen Jezebel who he fears,
He can hear the echo of the wind in the cave,
The roar of the angry flames,
Ashes filled his nostrils,
Damp wind catches at the back of my throat.

Emma Whitty (10)
North Baddesley Junior School

Autumn Canal

In my picture I can see
Shimmering water reflecting in the canal.
The roaring lion.
Autumn trees.
Running sheep in the sky
Rushing over the swift canal.
Barge boat sailing slow down the glossy water.

Stephanie White (11)
North Baddesley Junior School

The Tiger's Movement

In my picture I can see
Eyes of bright yellow and black.
In my picture I can see
Stripes of black and orange.
Tiger racing to find an end
Of a sunset so stripy and a bright bright yellow
Forcing his way through the touch and strong
Mysterious deep dark blue and turquoiseness.

Charlotte Ashworth (10)
North Baddesley Junior School

The Glowing Tiger

In my picture I can see,
A sunset glowing into the shining blue water,
Stripes of colour black and orange.

In my picture,
There is a tiger running in the clear glistening water,
Reflections shining into the light blue never-ending water.

In my picture I can see,
A tiger's tail swaying in the sunset,
The tiger rushing in the reflected calm water.

In my picture
Water is rushing and splashing about,
The tiger's eyes are glowing.

Natalie Harris (11)
North Baddesley Junior School

In My Picture I Can See

A man hiking up the rocks
Green slime climbing up the rocks
Water gushing down and angrily crashing against the waves
A Jacuzzi lays on top of the soft water
Water rising above the Jacuzzi
The soft woolly cotton wool fills the sky and hides
The gleaming golden sun
Rocks spying quietly to watch the noisy playful children
Water flowing by smoothly and whispering as it makes
A quiet, relaxing noise.

Sammie Whitty (10)
North Baddesley Junior School

My Worst Enemy

Once upon a rhyme, I found the biggest dime,
It could be very rare
Or maybe it belongs to that bear.
The bear walked towards me,
He looked very mad,
He took the big dime and I was very sad,
I tried to battle back,
But he threw me in a sack.
It turned out to be
That bear's my worst enemy.
His name is Dirty Dan,
And he's always threatening my nan.
I wish he'd leave me alone,
Or it would be good if he broke a bone.
Dan has always been dumb
And he has never stopped thinking
That he invented the thumb.
He took me to his house,
I never thought it would be as quiet as a mouse.
But what ever he does to me,
He will always be my worst enemy.

Curtis Sanderson (10)
Red Barn Primary School

No More Poems

Poems are the craze today,
Although they weren't yesterday.
All we do is sit and write,
Though it is not all right.
No more *poems!*

Christopher Kelly (10)
Red Barn Primary School

The TV Show: I'm A Celebrity Get Me Out Of Here!

They were in the jungle
And they had a royal rumble,
Peter won the fight,
So he lit a light.

Ant and Dec came to make their announcement,
First they said, 'I'm giving up sweets for Lent'
Mike had to go,
He said, 'I'll see you in a mo.'

Dianne was next and went to see Mike,
Riding there on her new mountain bike,
She was glad she only did one trial,
At least she was in the game a while.

Razor hated the rice and beans,
And he accidentally ripped his jeans,
Jennie had to sow them up,
While Razor drunk out of his cup.

Next Razor had to go,
All he said was, 'So,'
Johnny swore and walked out,
While he had a little shout.

Because Johnny had gone,
No one left that day, while the sun shone,
Alex Best left the camp next,
She had little votes by text.

Jordan is a model, but has little fans,
She used to collect cola cans,
The public decided to vote her out,
She knew she was going without a doubt.

Lord Brocket was a real man
And when he went he ran,
They all thought Lord B would win,
So they kicked each other in the shin.

In the final Peter left,
Across the bridge to Ant and Dec,
Kerry was crowned Queen of the jungle,
Her husband came and they had a mumble.

Goodbye Jennie you didn't stand a chance,
It must have hit you like a lance,
Kerry is now the leader,
She is quite a good reader.

Thomas Guildford (9)
Red Barn Primary School

The Monster Named Ki

There once was a monster named Ki,
Who always had a little cry,
He went up to space,
And looked at his face,
Then he cried and he cried and he cried!

One day he went to the beach,
And brought a soft peach,
He started to cry,
Then talked to his friend Mi,
And he lied and he lied and he lied!

After a long week,
He grew a long beak,
And had a long weep,
Leaving a puddle that was deep,
And he sighed and he sighed and sighed!

He now was 100 years old,
And always very cold,
He went to bed,
With his ted,
And he died and he died and he died!

Adam Spencer-Hicken (9)
Red Barn Primary School

My Family

M y mum is nice because she buys me sweets
Y ou are crazy as a yo-yo

F unny as a fish
A s gentle as a mouse
M ouse is like a rat
I n my house it is messy
L ong as a lion
Y ou are all nice.

Nathan Huitson (9)
Red Barn Primary School

Football Mad

F ootball is great
O thers think not
O thers are superb in defence
T igers are great in defence and up front
B ears amazing in goal
A ntelopes are rubbish in midfield
L eopards are the moody managers
L adybirds on the bench.

Bradley Elmes (10)
Red Barn Primary School

Seven Things I Love About Natalie

N aughty
A lways there
T alkative
A ttractive
L ovely
I rresistible
E xciting.

Adam Long (11)
Red Barn Primary School

Friendship

F ight for you
R un with you
I f you are hurt they help you
E nd something that has to be ended
N ice to you
D on't be rude to you
S tand up and help you
H elp you if you feel bad
I n a game they are on your side
P lay with you.

Blake Folgado (10)
Red Barn Primary School

Football

F ooty is the best
O n the ball
O h! It is a goal
T om took kick-off from the goal
B rilliant passing
A ll the people are going crazy
L ewis has the ball
L ucy blew the whistle for full-time.

Connor Blyth (9)
Red Barn Primary School

Monkey

M onkeys are silly
O ranges are for eating
N asty boys get smacked
K ites are for flying
E lephants eat eggs
Y oyos are for playing.

Samuel Wickham (9)
Red Barn Primary School

What!

Mum! Mum!
What!
What's for tea?
Just stop bugging me!

Dad! Dad!
What!
What are you doing for glee?
Just stop bugging me!

Sister! Sister!
What!
Why are you dressing for a ball?
Just stop bothering us all!

Brother! Brother!
What!
What are you doing with that hall?
For the last time stop bothering us all!

Keith Edwards (11)
Red Barn Primary School

My Teacher

My teacher sits in a chair
She takes the register then and there
And I seemed to have found
That she lazes around
Early in the morning.

My teacher plays with her hair
And everyone says she is rare
She shouts and moans
She wails and groans
Early in the morning.

Annabelle Phelan (11)
Red Barn Primary School

Swimming Fun

In I came
Armed with my goggles and swimming cap,
I tightened up my great goggles' strap.
I walked to the deep end and prepared myself,
Up went my arms with toes on the edge,
And go!
Bye to the floor said my toes,
And hello water said my head.

I'm in the water now, got 2 hours of fun,
Splashing and kicking fun all around,
Time goes fast, time to get out,
Got to go back to my troubles,
But oh no, where are my goggles?

Back in the water looking all around,
Where are my goggles? They have got to be found.
There!
Under the water eyes stinging red,
And got them!

Back to the surface gasping and sighing,
Got to get to the side and get out quick,
I changed in a hurry,
And waited for Mum.
Here she comes waving happily,
I got in the car and she said,
'Are you all right dear?'
And I replied, 'No!
My eyes are red,
And I've got water in my head!'

Megan Standen (11)
Red Barn Primary School

Friends

F riends are fun and helpful and they can be kind
R obots are OK but friends are better
I nsane, mad, funny, happy, that is what my friends are like
E nter your friend's house and your friend will enter yours
N asty people all about but my friends are not
D ogs and cats lots are not friends but mine are
S illy children are having fun.

Benjamin Davis (11)
Red Barn Primary School

My Pet Freddy

My cat Freddy will scratch you if he can
Every lady and every man
He will leer at everything, even other cats
But not when he's eating big, juicy rats
He will jump up and sleep on my feet
But not when he's on the dark, scary streets.

Elliot Elcock (10)
Red Barn Primary School

Stars

S ea is so shiny it shimmers in the sun
T he wind blows so hard it whistles through the air
A pples are so sweet, they always grow so well
R ed is the colour to say that you're mad
S ad is the thing that you would say is bad.

Ann-Marie Hinshelwood (9)
Red Barn Primary School

The Day I Saw Snow

I looked outside and I saw snow,
It looked really thin but it started to grow.

So I walked outside and made a snowball,
Then my sister walked out and she looked very tall.

I threw the snowball to my sister's belly,
Then I looked in the window and my mum was watching the telly.

I went in to go to bed,
I looked at my hands and they seemed very red.

The next day the snow was gone,
Out came the sun and it really shone.

Emily Seall (11)
Red Barn Primary School

Chocolate

I like chocolate that is lovely,
Dreamy, soft and creamy,
Chocolate that is melting, or chocolate that is white,
And I eat chocolate every day and night.
Oh look what is on my plate,
Chocolate, chocolate, chocolate.

James Goble (10)
Red Barn Primary School

Simile Poem

Penguins play on polar bears
Oranges are as orange as octopus
Everyone is as busy as bees
My mum is as silly as a slug.

Joseph Rinomhota (8)
Red Barn Primary School

Football Crazy

Adam's in midfield,
Bradley's at the back,
Curtis is the striker,
Defender got quite a whack.

Elliot is our right back,
Frankie is our manager,
George is on the bench,
Harry's quite a danger.

I like to score
Josh likes to slide,
Kieron likes to header,
Lee plays out wide.

Matt is quite greedy,
Nathan's quite hard,
Oliver takes free-kicks,
Peter shows red card.

Quinton plays on the left,
Robert plays in goal,
Samantha is our cheerleader,
Tom made a hole.

Ursula is quite skilful
Vincent is quite fast,
William is our fitness coach,
Xavier in a cast.

Yakubu hit the post
Zack then scored a *goal!*

Charlie Anderson (11)
Red Barn Primary School

Please!

Please Mum, please Mum
I've done all the things you said.
I've tidied up my bedroom
And I've also made my bed.

Please Mum, please Mum
Tonight I'll wash the dishes
I'll also hang the washing out
And help you feed the fishes

Please Mum, please Mum
Just give me a little treat
Maybe a bar of chocolate
Or a couple of sweets.

Please Mum!
Can I have a fiver?

Ryan Burrows (10)
Red Barn Primary School

Summer And Winter

Summer

I went in the car with my mother,
To go to the beach in summer
We had a good time
And drank some wine
And that was the end of my mother.

Winter

I went out to play in winter
All of a sudden I got a splinter
It really hurt
And ruined my skirt
And that was the end of my winter.

Kirsty Lloyd (11)
Red Barn Primary School

The Seasons

S ummer is great
U nder the sun
M e and my friends play
M e and my brother play in the pool
E ven my dog likes summer
R ain doesn't come.

W ind is fun, you stay up late
I n winter it is cold
N ever sun comes
T onight rain will fall
E veryone loves snow in winter
R ain comes in winter.

S pring is good
P lants start to die
R ain starts to come
I n the spring it is cold
N ever eat spring plants
G reat, spring is good.

A utumn is good
U nder the trees leaves fall down
T he leaves are red
U nder the trees you stay warm
M y mum says she likes autumn
N ever eat autumn's leaves.

Maisie Chambers (10)
Red Barn Primary School

Cracker (My Rabbit)

Running, jumping round and round
In the sun and on the ground
In the rain and on the drain
In the winter he's a sprinter
In the heat he burns his feet
But he's a great rabbit to have.

Roxanne Reeve (11)
Red Barn Primary School

My Pets - Dog And Cat

M ad as a mouse
Y ummy as a yoghurt

P ink as a panda
E arly as an earthworm
T all as a tiger
S pooky as a spider

D aft as a dog
O range as an octopus
G reat as Georgia

A ngry as an ant
N utty as a nut
D aft as a dinosaur

C rafty as a cat
A wful as an ant
T alking teachers.

Georgia-Mae Holloway (8)
Red Barn Primary School

Football Crazy

F ootball is so good
O h, he shoots and he scores
O h what a celebration by Beckham
T he crowd are going wild
B ut Nistlerooy jumps on him
A ll of the other teams are going to cry
L osers they're singing
L ots of goals are going in now

C razy game is going on
R ubbish toe punts by Giggs
A good free-kick by John O'Shea
Z igzag run by Gary Neville
Y ou are quite good O'Shea.

Connor Phipps (10)
Red Barn Primary School

Good Books

G ood books
O ur class loves reading books
O range and crazy books flying in the air
D irty books which eat people

B ooks that fly and attack
O h my God, what shall I do?
O h I will open this book
K neel down and open the book
S sssssnap!

Lincoln Pepall (9)
Red Barn Primary School

Football

F ootball mad
O n the spot
O ne-one is the score
T he crowd are bad
B all is under the foot
A ll the players are cheering
L osers!
L osers!

James Payne (9)
Red Barn Primary School

My Mates

M ad as my mum
Y ummy as a yoghurt

M y mate Matthew made maggots
A ngry Ann ate ants
T iny Tom took tea bags
E lly in England eats elephants
S illy sister is sausages.

Connor Morrison (8) & Tom Webb (9)
Red Barn Primary School

I'm A Celebrity, Get Me Out Of Here!

They were all having a good time,
Until Mike fell of the line,
Diane had to go,
Jennie was getting the flow.

Kerry needed a poo,
But there was a spider in the loo,
Peter and Lord B came to the rescue,
But were told to wait outside because Kerry was on the loo!

Jordan went to bed,
But had a visitor . . . Peter!
And she went all red.

Razor was third to go,
And John followed,
He said Jordan's career was a load of rubbish,
And he went off in a tish!

Peter made up some songs,
And Jordan sang along,
Ant and Dec came,
And said who was out of the game!

Kerry and Jordan were getting ready,
They didn't seem very steady,
They had a trial to do,
One glass of water and yucky foods too.

Alex had a trial,
Which would take her a while,
She had a phobia of snakes,
And she didn't have what it takes.

Now they've only got three,
I'm glad one of them's not me!

Kathryn Booth (9)
Red Barn Primary School

My Family And Pets

As silly as a snake
As busy as a bee
As boring as a bug
As nutty as a nut
As slow as a slug
As spooky as a spider
As friendly as a bee
As yummy as a yoghurt.

Connor Waring (9)
Red Barn Primary School

My Family And Pets

My cat is as catty as cocoa powder
My mum is as crazy as a crocodile
My dad is as dainty as a daisy
My cat is as cool as the cool air
My pets are like poppies
My dad is as strong as a dinosaur.

Nicole Mattravers (9)
Red Barn Primary School

Untitled

As strong as a stallion
As gentle as a goat
As fast as a ferret
As slow as a slug
As happy as a hamster
As silly as a Spaniel.

Ronny Chambers (9)
Red Barn Primary School

Untitled

As strong as a giant
As gentle as animals
As fast as a cheetah
As slow as a slug
As happy as the sunshine
As silly as a clown
As spooky as a spider
As scruffy as scrunched paper.

Carla Huitson (9)
Red Barn Primary School

The Writer Of This Poem . . .

(Based on 'The Writer of This Poem' by Roger McGough)

As strong as a snake
As gentle as a giggle
As fast as a fish
As slow as a snowflake
As happy as a hat
As silly as a struggle.

Jay Wake (8)
Red Barn Primary School

Family Football Mad

Mother in goal, brother in a hole
Father in defence, cousin on the bench
Sister in midfield, baby's off the field
Grandad in attack, nan on his back
Uncle making a bet, auntie stuck in the net
Other brother defending his mother
Oh Mother, you let in a goal!

James Milner (9)
Red Barn Primary School

Rain

In the rain you get wet,
If you dare you will sweat.

Run, run before you get wet,
Walk, walk, walk your pet.

Worms, worms come out in the rain,
Slugs, slugs are a pain.

Rebecca Masterson (11)
Red Barn Primary School

The Magic Box

(Based on 'Magic Box' by Kit Wright)

I will put in the box . . .
The eclipse I saw at midday,
The sound of a phone,
Fire springs from the bonfire.

I will put in the box . . .
The first person I ever heard talk,
The smell of pancakes,
The taste of Mars bars.

I will put in the box . . .
My imaginary friend,
The taste of cheese,
The smell of daffodils.

I will put in the box . . .
A tyrannosaurus-rex who lost his teeth,
A dinosaur riding a bike,
Beautiful flowers that smell disgusting.

Ashley Hyde (9)
St Anthony's Catholic Primary School, Fareham

The Magic Box
(Based on 'Magic Box' by Kit Wright)

I will put in my magic box . . .
The taste of hot turkey lying in your mouth,
The feeling of a snowflake melting in your hand,
Sunny sand sizzling your feet.

I will put in my magic box . . .
The smell of rose petals tickling your nose,
The last coin from the tooth fairy,
A piece of cool breeze on a summer's night.

I will put in my magic box . . .
A block of ice from the cold winter,
The last walking stick from my grandad,
A sip of the deep blue sea.

I will put in my magic box . . .
A spark of fire,
The present out of my cracker at Christmas,
My first baby toy.

My box is made out of sand
With nine carat gold sparkling in the night,
It has stands on it like dolphin tails.

I shall ski in my box on Mount Everest,
Then go to the bottom to have a rest
In my magic box.

Emily Zambra (9)
St Anthony's Catholic Primary School, Fareham

The Magic Box

(Based on 'Magic Box' by Kit Wright)

I will put in my box . . .
The sun setting over the sea,
The gates opening from Heaven with blazes of sun,
The snow falling in paradise.

I will put in my box . . .
The sounds of little birds chirping,
Baby animals playing with each other,
The waves crashing against the sand.

I will put in my box . . .
The smell of spring and summer air,
Fresh red roses,
Delicious, delicate daffodils.

I will put in my box . . .
Luscious, cold chocolate ice cream,
Melted chocolate,
Rainbow sweets.

I will put in my box . . .
Wishes that come true,
My gran alive,
Swimming with shining, shimmery dolphins.

I will put in my box . . .
Big, fat, pink pigs that fly with white wings and halos,
Angels snorting in pigsties,
Horses doing flicks,
Gymnastics being rode on.

My box is made out of gold, secrets and glitter with friendship,
Its hinges are made out of the rainbow.

I shall somersault in my box,
Landing on the thin, straight beam,
To then win a medal.

Abigail Prosser (9)
St Anthony's Catholic Primary School, Fareham

The Magic Box

(Based on 'Magic Box' by Kit Wright)

I will put in the box . . .
a fiery sun from Spain
the blue sea rolling upon a sunny coloured beach
and the lift-off of Apollo 13

I will put in the box . . .
the taste of sparkling water
and the taste of a grated cheese sandwich
with a lovely, luscious lollipop.

I will put in the box . . .
the touch of a dragon's scales
and water as warm as a full-on radiator
plus smooth, soft skin.

I will put in the box . . .
a dream of being a super hero
and flying a helicopter
also being a president.

I will put in the box . . .
the smell of freshly made crisp bread
and the smell of fresh fruit
plus salty water.

I will put in the box . . .
the sound of my mum singing
of rustling leaves
and the sound of 'Busted'.

My box is made of ice and a lock made of gold
that will be my box.

Christian Davison (8)
St Anthony's Catholic Primary School, Fareham

The Magic Box

(Based on 'Magic Box' by Kit Wright)

I will put in the box,
A tyrannosaurus-rex that has lost its left foot,
A cave man riding a skateboard,
A blue hedgehog with running trainers on.

I will put in the box . . .
A fox with two tails and a sword,
An octopus with two human legs,
A dog with sunglasses.

I will put in the box . . .
A fat man with a flying robot,
A man that can fly and fire energy waves,
A fish with a human face.

I will put in the box . . .
The smell of cooked bacon,
The taste of just baked cookies,
A dragon with a bad cold.

My box is painted with blue all over,
With a pitch-black ground and one white wall,
In the corners are pepperoni pizzas.

Conor Hurren (9)
St Anthony's Catholic Primary School, Fareham

The Magic Box

(Based on 'Magic Box' by Kit Wright)

I will put in the box . . .
A nice, big, fat Winnie the Pooh
Lovely colours - red and yellow
The sweet smell of honey.

I will put in the box . . .
The country of Turkey,
The sound of the chickens outside,
The taste of a cocktail drink.

I will put in the box . . .
A fun sleepover at my friend's house
The sound of my friends messing about
The taste of brown milk chocolate.

I will put in the box . . .
The touch of a blue river flowing under me
The sound of people having a picnic on the river bank
And the taste of fresh water.

My box is fashioned from pure gold with rubies and emeralds all over
And pure silver for the handle
And black dog paws on the lid.

Lucy Markham (8)
St Anthony's Catholic Primary School, Fareham

The Magic Box

(Based on 'Magic Box' by Kit Wright)

I will put in my box . . .
The first toy from a shop in Bath
The first tooth that came out of my mouth
A book that came out of wrapping paper.

I will put in my box . . .
The sound of my brother when he was a baby
A sound of a dog howling in the wind
The sound of everyone at a funfair.

I will put in my box . . .
The smell of the freshly cut grass
The smell of the food in the house
The smell of petrol at the petrol station.

I will put in my box . . .
The taste of pizza when I go to school
The taste of a chip made in McDonald's
The taste of salt that came from the sea.

I will put in my box . . .
A rabbit flying into my bedroom
A big pig with wings.

I will put in my box . . .
A baby playing golf and an old man in a cot.

My box is made out of unbreakable wood
With swirls on the sides and hearts on the top.

Lauren Andrews (8)
St Anthony's Catholic Primary School, Fareham

The Magic Box

(Based on 'Magic Box' by Kit Wright)

I will put in the box . . .
the first snowboarder I have seen,
the first cheer in a football match,
my brother's first gig.

I will put in the box . . .
the smell of chocolate ice cream,
the scent of bubble bath,
the smell of toffee.

I will put in the box . . .
the taste of lovely turkey,
the taste of syrup,
the taste of dark chocolate.

I will put in the box . . .
the dream of my gigantic monster truck,
the dream of me playing for Saints FC,
the dream of me diving in The Great Barrier Reef.

I will put in the box . . .
a dinosaur surfing in the sea,
and a surfer eating people.

My box is made of multicoloured jewels and platinum.

I will put in the box . . .
the golden hot sun and sky,
the green soft grass,
and the wavy blue sea.

William Fairman (8)
St Anthony's Catholic Primary School, Fareham

The Magic Box

(Based on 'Magic Box' by Kit Wright)

I will put in my box . . .
The lovely sight of a graceful gander,
Pretty gooses floating on the sparkling lake,
A horse galloping from field to field.

I will put in my box . . .
The lovely sound of a mobile phone's siren song,
The pretty sound of birds flying by,
The sound of beautiful safari music.

I will put in my box . . .
The fresh, fragrant smell of flowers,
The lovely smell of petrol from the petrol station,
The smell of delicious baked cookies lying on a plate.

I will put in my box . . .
The taste of cool chocolate,
The taste of lovely, sticky toffee pudding,
The taste of delicious chocolate mousses in a tub.

I will put in my box . . .
The dreams of a Chinese dragon,
The dreams of a cheese room filled with cheese.

My magic box is made from
Solid gold with purple and blue icicles for hinges,
It has a flowery surface top to bottom with light blue flowers.
The leaves have repetitive patterns and are green.

Bethany Woolford (9)
St Anthony's Catholic Primary School, Fareham

The Magic Box

(Based on 'Magic Box' by Kit Wright)

I will put in my box . . .
My first toy from my nana,
My very first tooth that fell out,
My very, very first curl on my head.

I will put in my box . . .
The first squeak of my guinea pig,
My dog's first bark,
My first sound when I was a baby.

I will put in my box . . .
The lovely smell of fireworks,
The spark of the bonfire,
The smell of the petrol at the petrol station.

I will put in my box . . .
The taste of Cadbury's chocolate,
The taste of chocolate chip ice cream,
The taste of spaghetti bolognese.

I will put in my box . . .
A huge swimming pool,
An enormous pool with dolphins in it to ride,
Winnie the Pooh.

I will put in my box . . .
A surfer running round a stable,
A horse surfing in the sea.

My box is made of wood with stickers on it.

Rachel Giles (8)
St Anthony's Catholic Primary School, Fareham

The Magic Box

(Based on 'Magic Box' by Kit Wright)

I will put in my box . . .
The delicious taste of an apple turnover,
The first time I heard a blackbird calling on a spring day,
And when I saw the velvety colour of the night sky
With all the sparkling stars.

I will put in my box . . .
A mouse catching a cat,
And a cat eating cheese in a mouse hole.

I will put in my box . . .
When I went to the London Eye and Buckingham Palace,
A scarecrow stuffed with straw riding by in his car,
Vroom, vroom - that's the noise he makes
As he drives over London Bridge.

My box is made of unbreakable cheese with a toffee lock.
The corners of my box are made of shiny steel,
The lid of my box is made of spaghetti,
And the inside of the box is made of lovely leather.

Zach Johnston (9)
St Anthony's Catholic Primary School, Fareham

The Magic Box

(Based on 'Magic Box' by Kit Wright)

I will put in the box . . .
a wave from the big blue sea,
the sharp, chirping of a bluebird,
the touch of a gentle fairy's wings.

I will put in the box . . .
the diamonds in a midnight sky,
the sweet smell of strawberries,
a tower from the Taj Mahal.

I will put in the box . . .
the strong taste of warm curry,
the smell of a rose's petal,
the first crack of thunder.

I will put in the box . . .
the touch of a rough piece of bark off a tree,
a commander wearing a tutu,
and a ballerina fighting in a war.

My box is fashioned with velvet and with diamonds on the top,
with catches that are gold and a lock with a ruby on.

Amelia Notley (8)
St Anthony's Catholic Primary School, Fareham

The Magic Box

(Based on 'Magic Box' by Kit Wright)

I will put in my box . . .
The first pony trek I had in Ireland,
The loudest bark from my dog when a visitor comes,
The last unicorn I saw gallop past my window on Easter night.

I will put in my box . . .
The smell of a cake baking in the oven,
The delicious taste and smell of chocolate,
And the lovely taste of caramel marshmallows and chicken.

I will put in my box . . .
Dreams of unicorns galloping into my room,
My dog walking on its two hind legs
And talking like a human.

I shall swim in my box . . .
On the great atlas and swim to home all in one hour.

My box is made of
Ice and is very fragile.

Freya Evershed (8)
St Anthony's Catholic Primary School, Fareham

The Magic Box

(Based on 'Magic Box' by Kit Wright)

I will put in my box . . .
The gentle breeze on a bright summer's day,
The colourful sunrise on the green hills,
And the flowing sea.

I will put in my box . . .
The sound of the sea devouring the sand,
The sound of the cat's miaow,
And the sound of the elephant's roar.

I will put in my box . . .
The smell of fresh bread,
A fish flying,
And a magpie swimming.

My box will be made from silver, stars and dragon's tails
And the clips will be fish's fins.

I shall skate in my box on the glittery ice
Till I have real victory!

Charlotte Stanton (8)
St Anthony's Catholic Primary School, Fareham

The Magic Box
(Based on 'Magic Box' by Kit Wright)

I will put in the box . . .
The look of an unwrapped mummy,
A fireball which is scorching,
A portal to 4D dimension.

I will put in the box . . .
The dream of seeing a spaceship destroy my sister,
The dream of a day when I will get a pet Komodo dragon,
The dream of riding a wild lion.

I will put in the box . . .
The smell of chicken korma,
The smell of fresh paper,
The smell of freshly smoked haddock.

I will put in the box . . .
The sound of a mouse clicking on an icon,
The sound of a foot crunching on a crisp autumn leaf,
The sound of a footballer kicking the ball hard.

My box is fashioned from velvet, rock and crystal
With swirls of bright colours on the lid
And scrolls on the corners
Its hinges are ¾ of a football.

Charlie Briant (9)
St Anthony's Catholic Primary School, Fareham

The Magic Box

(Based on 'Magic Box' by Kit Wright)

I will put in the box . . .
A very bright rainbow
The sour smell of lemon
The taste of dripping chocolate.

I will put in the box . . .
A red rose petal
The sunset over the bright blue sea
The sound of a baby crying.

I will put in the box . . .
The sound of a bluebird singing
The greasy smell of McDonald's
All the beautiful colours of the rainbow.

I will put in the box . . .
Golden steps that lead up to Heaven
A picture of the villa I stayed in at Portugal
The freezing feeling of holding snow.

My magic box is made of gold, silver and all kinds of metals
It has silver and gold stars that shine in the dark
The hinges are the finger joints of crocodiles.

Shauna Solomon (9)
St Anthony's Catholic Primary School, Fareham

The Magic Box

(Based on 'Magic Box' by Kit Wright)

I will put in the box . . .
A pet dragon with icy breath
And about 15 dolphins in a swimming pool in my back garden.

I will put in the box . . .
The smell of hot 'n' spicy pizza
And the lovely smell of candles which have just been blown out.

I will put in the box . . .
The taste of hot dogs
And the taste of cheese and ham omelettes.

I will put in the box . . .
A tramp with a crown
And a king living out in the streets.

My box is made of
Unbreakable metal which can only be broken by a spell.

Jordan Stanley (9)
St Anthony's Catholic Primry School, Fareham

The Magic Box

(Based on 'Magic Box' by Kit Wright)

I will put in my box . . .
A baby on a motor bike
A hell's angel sucking a dummy
The London Eye.

I will put in my box . . .
The laughter of my cheeky sister
The smell of apple crumble
The smashing smell of spaghetti.

I will put in my box . . .
The beautiful taste of rhubarb crumble
The horrible taste of salty water.

My box is made of burning fire
And freezing ice.

James Wallis (9)
St Anthony's Catholic Primary School, Fareham

The Magic Box

(Based on 'Magic Box' by Kit Wright)

I will put in my box . . .
The Queen's stunning dress from the Coronation,
A vision from the one place of God,
The sight of lovely clear water.

I will put in my box . . .
The sound of crashing waves on sunny Croyde Bay,
Hearing adults scream like babies,
Hearing babies shout like adults.

I will put in my box . . .
The scent of beautiful blooming roses,
The smell of smoky burning water,
The feel of icy cold fires.

I will put in my box . . .
The flavour of biscuits from Sweden,
A nibble of chocolate from Belgium,
A mouthful of snails from France.

I will put in my box . . .
The twinkling stars on a cold clear water,
The colour of black clouds on a bright day,
The round, full yellow moon.

I will put in my box . . .
The white sun that is pouring with rain,
The clouds that are as bright as Heaven,
The mouse that is purring like a cat,
The cat that is squeaking like a mouse.

I will put in my box . . .
A visit to the lovely Buckingham Palace,
Time on the beautiful Croyde Bay beach,
A trip to the busy towns of London.

William Piper (9)
St Anthony's Catholic Primary School, Fareham

Seasons

Summer is hot, summer is fun
Summer is fun for everyone
Summer is when you can go on the beach
And you definitely eat some peach.

Spring is bright, spring is a great sight
I like spring 'cause it is light
Every time I go out to play
Laughing and joking in every way.

Autumn makes leaves fall down
Leaves are golden and brown
I like autumn 'cause it's fun
But I don't like to run.

Winter is cold it makes you want to shiver
When I went down to the river
It was frozen
And so was I.

Millie Manchip (8)
St Paul's Catholic Primary School, Portsmouth

Working With The Band

Snowballs flying through the air,
People sitting feeling bare.
Refreshing cocoa for me to drink,
After that I sit and think.

Cold snowball coming my way,
Calling me to come and play.
Damp, frozen, freezing hands,
Icy, chilly snowflake going round the band.

Some time it will stop,
Then I better hurry up.
Now come on quickly together,
One more time and we can play in this weather.

Megan Holt (8)
St Paul's Catholic Primary School, Portsmouth

Summer

I love summer,
It's my favourite time of the year,
So I can go out for a swim
With my best friend Kim.

I love summer,
It's my favourite time of the year,
It's lovely and warm
With some cool breezes at dawn,
I love summer.

Tanya Bee (9)
St Paul's Catholic Primary School, Portsmouth

On Planet 20

On planet 20
The aliens went to a slime party
And had a pint of beer.
One alien had two and another had four.
Dom was the king who went down to Earth
And said, 'This is empty.'
He went back to planet 20.
He said, 'Here are the earthlings,'
And sent them back to Earth.

Charlotte Smith (9)
St Paul's Catholic Primary School, Portsmouth

When Children Ruled The World

Once there were children
Who took over the world
Chocolate, sweets, cookies and candy
Anything you can wish for
Grown-ups have an island of their own
When children ruled the world.

Callum Ardern (9)
St Paul's Catholic Primary School, Portsmouth

Busted

Busted hate school
But love their teachers
They're totally cool
With their excellent features

Charlie's the tallest
With Matt in the middle
James is the smallest
But they're all individual

Their music is rude
They play all night
They eat junk food
Till they give us a fright

They all hate mustard
But I don't care
I'll always love Busted
And their spiky hair.

Tom Smith (9)
St Paul's Catholic Primary School, Portsmouth

Football Final

Football final is today,
I've been saving since May.
Shall I buy a big coke,
Or shall I speak to a bloke?

Football final is 1-0,
I've been arrested by the 'Old Bill'.
See you next year,
When it comes near.

The good thing is
We have won the cup.

Brett Togwell (8)
St Paul's Catholic Primary School, Portsmouth

Noise Nicker

(Based on 'The Sound Collector' by Roger McGough)

I browsed around a pet shop,
In my tattered jeans and top.
Collected all the pet shop sounds,
And sealed them in a pot.

The dinging of the bell,
That hangs above the door.
The squeaking of a white mice,
And the guinea pig that gnaws.

The purrs of the kitten,
Curled up on a rug.
The barks from the animal,
That is called a dog.

The hissing of the untamed snake,
The parrot nattering:
'Polly want a cracker?'
And the till going ding, ding.

The clock ticking on the wall,
The hamster in his wheel.
And people saying to the dog,
'Very good mutt, heal.'

The shopkeeper blah-blahing,
Tellin' kids 'bout pets.
The assistants trying to catch,
Fish with fishing nets, *splash!*

Ladies screaming at rats,
As the rats run wild.
The children are all screaming too,
Except one tiny child.

Callum Veale (9)
St Paul's Catholic Primary School, Portsmouth

The River's Flow

Rivers flow go, go, go
Down the hill it's really not slow
Twisting and turning as it's passing trees
Winding its way through mountain to the seas.

The rushing rivers down the hill
It passes the daffodils
The rocky cliff is very loose
It is really no use.

It finally reaches the sea
The waves are buried in the open sea.

Charlie Cooper (9)
St Paul's Catholic Primary School, Portsmouth

Busted Year 3000

Busted are cool, we think they rule.
They hated their school and they have a pool.
Charlie's the tallest and James is the smallest,
Matt's in the middle like hey middle diddle.

Charlie got through by an audition
And then went on a mission.
Matt said, 'Blimey isn't he tall.'
Charlie said to James, 'Crikey you're small.'

Jessica Warren (8)
St Paul's Catholic Primary School, Portsmouth

My Family

Mummy is for helping me
Matt is for bullying me
I am for being kind
Daddy is for cuddling me when I am sad.

Holly Duckett (8)
St Paul's Catholic Primary School, Portsmouth

The Pet Sound Collector

(Based on 'The Sound Collector' by Roger McGough)

I browsed around the pet shop today
In my tattered jeans and top
Collected all the pet shop sounds
And sealed them in a pot.

The ringing of the telephone
The rustling of the straw
The rattling of the shopping trolley
The swooshing of the automatic door.

The tweeting of the cockatiel
The barking of the dog
The miaowing of the cat
The ribbit of a frog.

Sarrah Agulan (9) & Jack Wilkes (10)
St Paul's Catholic Primary School, Portsmouth

Football

Football, football
Little funny game
Everybody likes it
Teams are England and India.

Oh dear, who will win?
England scores a goal
India did too
They are winning
Football fans chanting.

Then there was a player
Who kicked the ball
India wins.

Kevin Johnson (8)
St Paul's Catholic Primary School, Portsmouth

Pet Noise Pincher

(Based on 'The Sound Collector' by Roger McGough)

I browsed around the pet shop today,
In my tattered jeans and top,
Collected all the pet shop sounds,
And sealed them in a pot.

The swishing of the doors,
The chattering of the children,
The gulping of fish in their tanks,
As the shop assistant fills them.

The nibbling of the hamsters,
The barking of the pup.
The squealing of guinea pigs,
And the tick-tock of the clock.

The hissing of the snakes,
The squawking of the parrot,
The gulping of the fish,
The rabbits asking for a carrot.

The miaowing of the kittens,
The purring of the cat,
But in this pet shop,
There are no bats.

The creeping of the mice and rats,
The ringing of the till,
All children saying wow,
Including the girl called Jill.

Lucy Catterall (9)
St Paul's Catholic Primary School, Portsmouth

Sound Stealer!

(Based on 'The Sound Collector' by Roger McGough)

I browsed through a pet shop today,
In my tattered jeans and top,
Collected all the pet shop sounds,
And sealed them in a pot.

The swooshing of the doors,
The purring of the cat,
The nattering of the shopkeeper,
As he takes off his coat and hat.

The growling of the dog,
The tick-tocking of the clock,
The hissing of the snakes,
I've collected these and it's only 10 o'clock!

The 'aaahing' of the children,
The pointing of the grannies,
There's toddlers in push chairs,
And even some nannies.

The bubbling of the fish tank,
The squeaking of the guinea pigs,
The tinging of the till,
The scraping noise when dogs start to dig!

The squeaking of the parrots,
The rustling of the rats,
The 'eeeking' of the mice,
This pet shop has everything except bats!

Sean Burby (10) & Carmen Langworthy (10)
St Paul's Catholic Primary School, Portsmouth

The Pet Shop

(Based on 'The Sound Collector' by Roger McGough)

I browsed around a pet shop today
In my tattered jeans and top
Collected all the pet shop sounds
And sealed them in a pot.

The squawking of the parrots
The rabbits munching on their carrots
The gulping of the fish as they swim around their tank
The dinging of the till collecting money for the bank.

Shelby Chitwood (10) & Lloyd Conner (9)
St Paul's Catholic Primary School, Portsmouth

Wakey! Wakey!

As the old milk bottle cart rattles lazily down the road,
The sun seems to chase it,
Men in dressing gowns
Open the doors and collect the milk.

As the swings creak,
Dogs bark
And birds chirp - as the sun
Rises over the barn.
Children arrive, play and laugh.

Early morning, the sun and skaters arrive together
BMXs shimmering in the sun,
As shiny as a mirror
As energetic as a cheetah.

The ferries start to emerge out of the bed of mist
With a foghorn, like a tired giant's yawn.

Niall Anderson (10)
St Swithun's RC Primary School, Southsea

Seasons

Winter
Winter dawn -
Baby robins searching for food
Fires roaring to keep people warm

Summer
Summer sunsets -
Children shouting to their mums for drinks
People going for an afternoon walk
On the warm sand.

Spring
Spring mid-morning -
Bunnies hopping
Flowers popping.

Autumn
Autumn afternoons -
Hear dead leaves crunching -
Fires burning.

Brendan Keegan (10)
St Swithun's RC Primary School, Southsea

Personification Day

That was the day
When the trees did a slow waltz.
When the wind screeched for help
When the windows shook with fear.

That was the day,
When the leaves swam in the murky puddles,
When the puddles rippled in the wind.

Jessica Moore (11)
St Swithun's RC Primary School, Southsea

I Want To Paint

I want to paint
A fat greyhound;
Too lazy to get up.

I want to paint
A hungry horse;
Hiccuping hilariously.

I want to paint
A green gate;
Falling like snow off a mountain.

I want to paint
The taste of a hot apple pie;
Emerging from creamy custard.

I want to paint
The memory;
Of my grandad's last smile.

Victoria Hopkins (10)
St Swithun's RC Primary School, Southsea

It's Not Fair

I knew what my mum would say
When I said I was going out.
She told me too many times
I wanted to scream and shout.

She told me one time too many,
'Mum, I know!' I would say,
But that would never stop me
From kissing Jess and Jenny.

When the boys came out to play
I really did run away!

Lucy Hennigan (11)
St Swithun's RC Primary School, Southsea

An Orc's Sack

A couple of arrows stolen from a
man's body, used to pierce the
flesh of Mankind.

A bow created from rotten oak
to fire arrows.

Treasure seized from the enemy
for power and patience.

A sword used for close combat
made from a fellow mate's bone.

A shield crafted from fire
and steel.

Flesh from a man's body
used for food.

Charlie John Gardener (10)
St Swithun's RC Primary School, Southsea

Personification Poem

That was the day
The wind puffed its winter air
When the puddles splashed the children.

That was the day
When the windows shivered in the icy breeze,
When the leaves swept across the playground.

That was the day
When the trees rested their branches,
When the trees grasped on to their leaves.

Victoria Reeves (10)
St Swithun's RC Primary School, Southsea

Wind

That was the day
When the wind grabbed my hand,
Soared through my face
With a wink in her eye.
A flash of light
It disappeared out of sight.

That was the day
When the wind said, 'Hello!'
A howl from the air
Not from the snow.

That was the day
When the wind glanced at me
A smile of tears then
A splash of glee.

That was the day I remember
So well, when the wind
Said, 'Hello!'
And a tear just fell.

Katie Jones (10)
St Swithun's RC Primary School, Southsea

Personification Day

That was the day
When the windows spied
When the tree wailed

That was the day
When the plants did the cancan.
When the trees played tag with the leaves.

That was the day
When the wind whistled
When the wires shivered.

Charlotte Tait (11)
St Swithun's RC Primary School, Southsea

Playground

That was the day
When the trees crinkled with old age,
When the bins rumbled like a tummy in hunger.

That was the day
When the leaves cried in the darkness
When the bench spoke like death.

That was the day
When the wind whispered sadness,
When the windows glared at your every move.

That was the day
When the puddles gurgled with misery,
When the wires whipped the icy wind.

Elisabeth Sarah Welfare (10)
St Swithun's RC Primary School, Southsea

Seasons

Winter, evening
Snow falls, glistening white
Robins sing, charmingly fly.

Summer afternoon,
Bare legs running along the road
People are munching and crunching.

Early autumn
Footballers on the pitch
The ball ricocheted as it hit the post.

Spring lambs growing,
Grass waking, eggs cracking.

Patrick Symonds (10)
St Swithun's RC Primary School, Southsea

Portsmouth Is Sleeping

The sky
is darkening. The
wind is blowing and
all the lights are showing.

All of Portsmouth
is fast asleep except for
the dancers down the street.

Misha Sugrue-Gee (11)
St Swithun's RC Primary School, Southsea

Dawn In Southsea

Down at the skatepark,
the gentle clatter of skateboards.
Teenagers sitting down to take
a break from the excitement.

Sunrise at the precinct,
busy shoppers drifting like a log down a river,
slowly passing shoppers by.

Clay Thompson (11)
St Swithun's RC Primary School, Southsea

Winter

That was the night when the wind snapped
and the frost bit at my nose.
The bare trees stared coldly at me,
Winter lay around.
Branches grabbing at my clothes
as the deadly wind made no sound.

Aden Thomas Flannagan (10)
St Swithun's RC Primary School, Southsea

The Writer Of This Poem

(Based on 'The Writer Of This Poem' by Roger McGough)

The writer of this poem is
As funny as a red-nosed clown.
Speedy like a cheetah.
I am a galloping horse,
As mad as a crazy ghost.

As scary as a blood-sucking bat,
Chatty, like a pop chat show.
I am a clock
Brown like a loveable dog.

The writer of this poem is a clock
And she likes it when it goes tick-tock.

Olivia Wood (9)
The Crescent Primary School

The Writer Of This Poem

(Based on 'The Writer Of This Poem' by Roger McGough)

The writer of this poem is
As beautiful as a silvery diamond
Is like a flower in the sun
As blonde as the yellow sand
Is like the sunlight shining over

Eyes blue-green like the grass
And the sky but mostly green
Skin as pale as the light

The writer of this poem is a flower
And it does not like it when it showers.

Laura Newman (8)
The Crescent Primary School

The Writer Of This Poem

(Based on 'The Writer Of This Poem' by Roger McGough)

The writer of this poem is
As crafty as a cheeky monkey,
Enjoys maths, like a professor.
Dances in the disco like a groovy chick
Is a funky dance mat on the TV.

I am as funny as a laughing clown on stilts,
I am a golden sunset,
My eyes sparkle like the blue sea,
Hair as short as dog's fur.

The writer of this poem is a light
Which never actually likes to come out at night.

Charmaine Ivermee (8)
The Crescent Primary School

The Writer Of This Poem

(Based on The Writer Of This Poem by Roger McGough)

The writer of this poem is
As funny as a joke book
Is like a cheeky monkey
Is a swimming fish
With a runny nose like a sweaty dog

Like a greedy monkey
As silly as a blind mouse

The writer of this poem is a pool
Who likes to read and write at school.

Callum Moore (8)
The Crescent Primary School

The Writer Of This Poem

(Based on 'The Writer Of This Poem' by Roger McGough)

The writer of this poem is
A tennis racquet,
As chattery as an annoying parrot,
Sleeps like a wise owl at night.
I'm a long-haired rabbit.

As sleek as a disguised slithery snake watching
her luscious prey,
I am a violin whose strings make a beautiful soft sound,
Sings like a stressed cat being trodden on.
I am a golden sunset folding into the fluffy clouds.

The writer of this poem is a flower,
When it comes to poetry she has a lot of power.

Zoe Handley-Greaves (8)
The Crescent Primary School

The Writer Of This Poem

(Based on 'The Writer Of This Poem' by Roger McGough)

The writer of this poem is
As freckly as a cheetah
Is like a flower, smiling at the sun
As friendly as a cat
Is like a shiny lollipop
As smart as a wizard

The writer of this poem is
As quiet as a daisy
Is like an artist
Hair is an orange.

Krissy Donohue (9)
The Crescent Primary School

The Writer Of This Poem

(Based on 'The Writer Of This Poem' by Roger McGough)

The writer of this poem is
As sneaky as a hungry caterpillar
Is like a cheeky monkey
Is a swimming shark, hunting for food
With sharp teeth like vampires

As shy as a butterfly
Is like a bright star
I am a happy holiday
She sometimes feels upset

The writer of this poem is a moon
And she'll come out and play very soon.

Shaneece Waller Adams (8)
The Crescent Primary School

The Writer Of This Poem

(Based on 'The Writer Of This Poem' by Roger McGough)

The writer of this poem is
As sleepy as a brown owl
Which sleeps all night
In a safe and cosy bed

As fast as a lion
Zooming across the field
As smelly as a red rose
As green as a bush

The writer of this poem is a rabbit
And she's got a really bad habit.

Abbie Marie Humphries (8)
The Crescent Primary School

The Writer Of This Poem

(Based on 'The Writer Of This Poem' by Roger McGough)

The writer of this poem is
As sleek as a sprinting cheetah,
Intelligent like a mad scientist,
As sneaky as a black panther,
I am a flying cricket ball.

As rough as a charging rhinoceros
Rumbling towards the dangerous offender.
I am a hissing cat crouched to
Pounce onto a squeaking mouse.
Funny like a joking clown with a
Sparkling bright red nose,
I am a zooming aeroplane diving,
Twisting and turning
Swooping into land.

The writer of this poem is a star
And he'll be driving a brand new car.

Thomas Dodson (9)
The Crescent Primary School

The Writer Of This Poem

(Based on 'The Writer Of This Poem' by Roger McGough)

The writer of this poem is
Happy as a hilarious clown
Is like a leaping, cheeky, energetic monkey
I am as blonde as a golden boiling sun
With a nose and a smiling mouth
The writer of this poem is a twinkling star
Who likes to play with his
Remote control car.

Daniel Cardinal (9)
The Crescent Primary School

The Writer Of This Poem

(Based on 'The Writer Of This Poem' by Roger McGough)

The writer of this poem is as
Cheeky as a mischievous pixie
Loud, like a noisy gorilla
Naughty, like a sneaky goblin

I am a peaceful, relaxing holiday
Zooming like lightning
Dodging like fire
I am a Pokémon

The writer of this poem is a star
Who wants to drive a bright red car.

Stephen Coles (8)
The Crescent Primary School

The Writer Of This Poem

(Based on 'The Writer Of This Poem' by Roger McGough)

The writer of this poem is
As shy as a timid butterfly
Hungry like an enormous elephant
Travels like a pouncing hare
I am a galloping horse

I am a twirling dance
As quiet as a searching mouse, looking for its food
As funny as a joke book making everyone laugh
As clumsy as a colourful clown

The writer of this poem is a sunset
And she does not like to get wet.

Elizabeth Wyatt (9)
The Crescent Primary School

The Writer Of This Poem

(Based on 'The Writer Of This Poem' by Roger McGough)

The writer of this poem is
A battling football,
As cheeky as a banana-eating chimpanzee,
Chattering like a colourful parrot.
I am a chocolate bar.

I am a cobra, poised to pounce, sliding in disguise,
I always keep my word like a very reliable person does.
I am a sprinting cheetah zooming across the open land,
My sparkling eyes shining green, like an emerald.

The writer of this poem is a star
And he likes a lot of chocolate bars.

Luke Blackburn (9)
The Crescent Primary School

The Writer Of This Poem

(Based on 'The Writer Of This Poem' by Roger McGough)

The writer of this poem is
As magical as a sleek unicorn
Travels like a cold smooth ice cream.
I am a leaping dance
I am a twinkling song

As funny as a laughing joke book
I am a red, red, rose; smoother than a fluffy cloud
I am a golden sunset shining on the horizon
As comfy as a leather suite smothered with cushions

The writer of this poem is a sunset
And she sometimes get a little upset.

Maisie James (8)
The Crescent Primary School

The Writer Of This Poem

(Based on 'The Writer Of This Poem' by Roger McGough)

The writer of this poem is
As tiny as a shiny tadpole
Is like a chatty parrot
As loud as an elephant
With grey skin, like leather

As shy as a butterfly
Is scary as a tiger jumping out at its prey
As loud as a dinosaur's feet
With gigantic footprints like elephant's feet

The writer of this poem is a star
She loves to explore near and far.

Abigail Wright (8)
The Crescent Primary School

The Writer Of This Poem

(Based on 'The Writer Of This Poem' by Roger McGough)

The writer of this poem is
As groovy as a disco diva
Playful like a baby kitten
Enjoys books like a writer
I am a book of mysteries.

I am a dance mat
As magic as a magician casting spells of wonder
Looks like a fluffy teddy bear, ready to be hugged
I am a golden sunset.

The writer of this poem is a rabbit
Who has all sorts of different kinds of habits.

Lorna Collins (8)
The Crescent Primary School

The Writer Of This Poem

(Based on 'The Writer Of This Poem' by Roger McGough)

The writer of this poem is
As slow as an elderly elephant,
I am a playful kitten
I am a greedy pig scoffing my food down,
When I am annoyed I behave like a disobedient toddler.

I am a beautiful unicorn sprinting wildly in the breeze,
Loves art like a perfectionist artist painting a peaceful
relaxing picture of the deep blue sea.
Inside my head, ticking away is a brain,
as brainy as a wise owl.
Cooking in the oven, I am a chocolate brownie, turning brown.
The writer of this poem is a flower
so she will lose a petal every hour.

Samantha Tait (9)
The Crescent Primary School

The Writer Of This Poem

(Based on 'The Writer Of This Poem' by Roger McGough)

As reliable as a trustworthy friend
I am a bar of chocolate
Enjoys school like an intelligent tick
Smiles like friends reunited

As poetic as a well-known perfection author
Laughs like a crooked evil witch mixing stew
I am an everlasting flower blooming while people
Enjoy music like a top band with huge fans

The writer of this poem is a tick
So she couldn't play a trick or take the mick.

Shireena Frederick (8)
The Crescent Primary School

The Writer Of This Poem

(Based on 'The Writer Of This Poem' by Roger McGough)

The writer of this poem is
As friendly as a tame hamster
I am a glowing sunset,
Devours books like buttery popcorn
As kind as an old woman.

I am a wispy dance, floating gracefully in the sky,
Clean like a window, glistening in the sun.
Talkative like a parrot, chatting to its owner,
As brainy as an open book, waiting to read.
The writer of this poem is a clock,
She will never cease writing, till the clock decides to stop.

Madeleine Hobbs (9)
The Crescent Primary School

The Writer Of This Poem

(Based on 'The Writer Of This Poem' by Roger McGough)

The writer of this poem
As clean as a sparkly whistle
Spooky like a ghost in the dark
I am a galloping horse.

As quiet as a tiptoeing mouse
Shy like a new girl
As nice as a lollipop lady
I am a traveller in the wild wind.

The writer of this poem is a flower
And she remains there every hour.

Abbie Stevens (8)
The Crescent Primary School

The Writer Of This Poem

(Based on 'The Writer Of This Poem' by Roger McGough)

The writer of this poem is
As beautiful as a shiny butterfly
Is like a black and white zebra
As fast as a furry lion
Is like a dancing daisy

As quiet as the light grass
Is like a kind, nice person.

Kanesha Agard (8)
The Crescent Primary School

The Writer Of This Poem

(Based on 'The Writer Of This Poem' by Roger McGough)

As good as a boy playing football
As beautiful as a blossom
She is fantastic at maths but bad at English
With a shy, friendly smile like the sun peeping
From behind a cloud.

The writer of this poem,
I'm sure you will agree,
Is completely wonderful - it's me!

Emma Baxter (8)
The Crescent Primary School

The Writer Of This Poem

(Based on 'The Writer Of This Poem' by Roger McGough)

The writer of this poem is
As happy as a hilarious king
Is like an old smashed pavement
Cramped like an eggshell
With a crack so big like a tree trunk
Is a rat who has a friendly bat.

Jake Herbert Peatroy (8)
The Crescent Primary School

The Writer Of This Poem
(Based on 'The Writer Of This Poem' by Roger McGough)

The writer of this poem
Who is as beautiful as a
Wonderful princess
A brilliant dancer like
Britney Spears, also the
Greatest singer.

As clever as the latest computer
As lovely as a mirror, but very vain
Eyes like sparkling, clear blue water.

The writer of this poem,
As you have read
Is as excellent as can be -
That's if you agree!

Lottie Jarvis (8)
The Crescent Primary School

The Writer Of This Poem
(Based on 'The Writer Of This Poem' by Roger McGough)

The writer of this poem is
As clean as a sparkling floor,
Cheeky as a red-nosed clown
I am a galloping horse in the wild
Safe like my cosy bed

Yellow like a tall sun in the sunset
As beautiful as a shaded rainbow
Shy, like a neurotic cat
Smiley like a cat when she is happy

The writer of this poem is a horse
She likes eating carrots of course.

Nicole Watson (9)
The Crescent Primary School

The Writer Of This Poem

(Based on 'The Writer Of This Poem' by Roger McGough)

Is as crazy as a wild horse which
Goes mental at a rodeo
Is as strange as a goldfish
In a tree
Its hair is ginger like autumn leaves
With lovely eyes as hazel
As a polished nut
As smart as the latest computer
As thin as bacon
As funny as a clown
As tall as the London Bridge
With a nose like a bumpy hill
The writer of this poem
I'm sure you'll agree
Is as smart as can be!

Tyler Rossi (8)
The Crescent Primary School

The Writer Of This Poem

(Based on 'The Writer Of This Poem' By Roger McGough)

Is as strong as a crane, which is *gigantic*
As powerful as a giant body builder,
More handsome than a model
Bigger than a colossal animal.

Rougher than a gang member,
Cooler than the world's strongest man
With a horrible smile like a grumpy man,
His bold, brown eyes are shining acorns.

The writer of this poem
I'm sure you'll agree,
Is as cool as he could possibly be!

Jack Ibbs (9)
The Crescent Primary School

The Writer Of This Poem

(Based on 'The Writer Of This Poem' by Roger McGough)

The writer of this poem
Is as handsome as James Bond
And as rich as Robbie Williams
He is as cool as the greatest spy ever
Who goes on a mission

As smart as the latest computer that can tell
What's 100385 x 34578966!
But as clumsy as a clown, in town
Thick brown hair like the colour of a grizzly bear
Sweet as sugar
Cheeks like an upside-down juicy strawberry
And cheeky, like a monkey.

The writer of this poem
I'm sure you'll agree
Is the wonderful, fantastic Jamie!

Jamie Edwards (9)
The Crescent Primary School

The Writer Of This Poem

(Based on 'The Writer Of This Poem' by Roger McGough)

Is as smart as a mathematician,
She is funny like a clownfish.
But sometimes as loud as a Sergeant Major
Who is shouting on parade
But she is bossy like an officious teacher.

Her lips are like raspberries
With dark blue eyes which look like
A stormy sea
Brown hair like a grizzly bear
With a nose like a strawberry.

The writer of this poem -
Which you have read,
I am as comfortable as a bed!

Samantha Walls (9)
The Crescent Primary School

The Writer Of This Poem

(Based on 'The Writer Of This Poem' by Roger McGough)

Is as crazy as a wild horse which charges away
All day long.
Is as dumb as a goldfish,
His hair is as spiky as a hedgehog
With eyes as bright as the deep blue sea.
As handsome as John Wayne and
As smart as an old computer.

As strange as a penguin
But as vicious as a sabre-toothed tiger.
As funny as a thunder storm
As tough as Kangaroo Jack and
As fast as a Grand Prix car.
As thin as a slice of ham
As tall as the tallest tower.

The writer of this poem
I'm sure you'll be surprised.
Is absolutely fantastic unless of course he lied!

Ben Tyrrell (8)
The Crescent Primary School

The Writer Of This Poem

(Based on 'The Writer Of This Poem' by Roger McGough)

The writer of this poem
Is as clever as a scientist.
As fast as lightning, which races across the sky.
As tricky as a mouse escaping from a cat.
As strong as a mighty bull charging round a field.

His eyes are blue like a whale's back
He could cause pandemonium, alone.

The writer of this poem
I'm sure you will agree
Is as amazing as it is possible to be!

Benjamin Whiteside (9)
The Crescent Primary School

The Writer Of This Poem

(Based on 'The Writer Of This Poem' by Roger McGough)

The writer of this poem
Is as fast as a jet-propelled Ferrari
As cool as the amazing James Bond -
Who is facing a deadly enemy
He is cleverer than a new computer
As sly as the most excellent spy.

As tall as the tallest Red Wood
He is as handsome as the most famous pop star ever
Who has a brilliant hairdo.
With his brown, gloomy eyes
Which stare down at you like a bear.

The writer of this poem,
I'm sure you will agree,
Is the wonderfully fantastic me!

Robert Jones (8)
The Crescent Primary School

The Writer Of This Poem

(Based on 'The Writer Of This Poem' by Roger McGough)

The writer of this poem
Is as serene as a princess
Who waits for her Prince Charming
With her long, flowing hair which streams
Like Rapunzel's

Her friendly smile talks to the animals like Snow White
Her blush is a delicate glass slipper,
As gloriously beautiful as the ferocious beast is ugly.

The writer of this poem,
To see this I'm sure you won't fail,
Is just caught up in a fairy tale!

Lauren Andrews (8)
The Crescent Primary School

The Writer Of This Poem

(Based on 'The Writer Of This Poem' by Roger McGough)

The writer of this poem
Is as beautiful as a wonderful butterfly
With smooth, brown, flat hair like Black Beauty.
Not so clever as an amazing computer.
Remembers nearly everything about maths
Like a calculator.

Her smile, which is like a lovely bright day, is happy
On her face are a few freckles, like an ellipsis.
Kind, like a fairy godmother,
As quiet as a walk through the forest.

The writer of this poem
I'm sure you'll agree
Is as clever as can be.

Amy Burley (9)
The Crescent Primary School

The Writer Of This Poem

(Based on 'The Writer Of This Poem' by Roger McGough)

Is a clumsy, crazy clown, who leaps
Around, all day.
As hilarious as a joke book
But that's just him.

His hair is as smooth as a pebble,
His cheeks are like speckled eggs,
Which stand out like bold letters on his face.
His eyes are deep chocolate
Melting in the sun,
His ears are like a monkey's - sticking out.

The writer of this poem,
I'm sure you'll agree,
Is as crazy as a wallaby!

Daniel Flux (9)
The Crescent Primary School

The Writer Of This Poem

(Based on 'The Writer Of This Poem' by Roger McGough)

The writer of this poem
Who is weaker than a tiny feather.
As clever as the latest calculator,
As funny as an amazing comedian,
Who has people crying with laughter.

Is terribly faster than a zooming cheetah
Speeding by,
As beautiful and handsome as James Bond
With a smile like a sunny day.
He is greedier than a giant pig
Snuffling in the mud.
His eyes are like a sparkling blue sea.

The writer of this poem,
I'm sure you'll agree,
Is as wonderful as a wallaby.

Sam Broadhurst (9)
The Crescent Primary School

The Writer Of This Poem

(Based on 'The Writer Of This Poem' by Roger McGough)

The writer of this poem,
Is as clever as a story writer.
As beautiful as a colourful butterfly.
She has pretty hair like a princess with long hair,
As loud as a scary lion.

As funny as a dopey clown,
Sleeps like a wriggly, shaky bear,
As helpful as a lollipop lady.

The writer of this poem,
You might agree with me,
Is as nice as a girl could possible be!

Katie Humphreys (8)
The Crescent Primary School

The Writer Of This Poem

(Based on 'The Writer Of This Poem' by Roger McGough)

The writer of this poem
Is as crazy as a running
Bandicoot, which is very fast.

As playful as a little bunny
Skipping cheerfully in the grass,
Like a tall elf with pointy ears,
Her flowing hair like a horse's mane.

Her artistic hands itching to grab
Hold of a pencil,
Her eyes glowing like cat's eyes
Glowing in the darkness.

The writer of this poem with her
Greek-coloured eyes
When you meet you'll be
In for a surprise.

Madeleine June Kenrick (8)
The Crescent Primary School

The Writer Of This Poem

(Based on 'The Writer Of This Poem' by Roger McGough)

The writer of this poem
Is as lovely as a bunch
Of spring flowers,
As quiet as a mouse,
Who eats cheese all day.
With wavy hair like the tranquil sea.

Her eyes are hazel-coloured pearls,
Her hair is brown with blonde streaks in it,
With white sparkling teeth,
Her smile is as bright as the sun.

The writer of this poem,
I'm sure you will agree,
Is as quiet as can be.

Hayley Kellaway (8)
The Crescent Primary School

The Writer Of This Poem

Based on 'The Writer Of This Poem' by Roger McGough)

The writer of this poem
Who is as annoying as a
Crazy chimpanzee.
Is as wonderfully clever as the
Latest calculator
And as generous as Father Christmas.

His flat hair is a burned hedgehog,
Which sticks out like a nutty professor's hair.
As mathematical as Einstein calculating a formula,
His eyes are a dark, scary night,
Glowing with intelligence.

The writer of this poem,
I'm sure you'll agree,
Is as wonderful as the dark blue sea.

Nick Chan (9)
The Crescent Primary School

The Writer Of This Poem

(Based on 'The Writer Of This Poem' by Roger McGough)

The writer of this poem is
As poor as a mum
Has short blonde brown hair
Like velvet.

Sometimes he is as vicious
As a dog
As small as a god,
As clever as a computer.
His eyes are like green grass.

The writer of this poem,
I'm sure you'll agree,
Is as stupid as can be!

Michael Turner (8)
The Crescent Primary School

The Writer Of This Poem
(Based on 'The Writer Of This Poem' by Roger McGough)

The writer of this poem
Is as playful as a lively brown puppy
Who chews all day.
Has flaxen hair, which is a river of
Sparkling gold, flowing over her shoulders.
As quiet as a silent, orange goldfish
Which swims all day long.

With eyes of shining blue pearls
Peeping out of the shell,
Her body is like a speedy cheetah
Stalking its prey,
She is as beautiful as a brown spotted fawn.

The writer of this poem,
I'm sure you now know,
Is as quick as a shy, rare doe.

Kim Lloyd (8)
The Crescent Primary School

The Writer Of This Poem
(Based on 'The Writer Of This Poem' by Roger McGough)

As pretty as a sunflower which is colourful, even delicate
Is like a funny, clumsy hen
As brilliant as a computer
As fit as a gym

Who is a great footballer with the Golden Boot
As fast as a galloping horse
With a beautiful smile like the sunset

Her hair smells like delicious strawberries

The writer of this poem
I think you can see
Is wonderful me!

Charlie White (8)
The Crescent Primary School

Kennings Dog

Cat chaser
bone taker
basket sleeper
cat creeper
doggy paddler
paperwork muddler
paw licker
tail flicker
messy dribbler
flowerbed fiddler.

Toby Hudson (10)
Wallop CP School

Kennings Cat

Fence leaper
long sleeper
ball chaser
tail flicker
fish eater
mouse fetcher
cat fighter
fur licker
food pincher
bad hisser.

Emma Hodges (10)
Wallop CP School

Short Visit, Long Stay

The school trip was a special occasion
But we never reached our destination
Instead of the zoo
I was locked in the loo
On an M62 Service Station.

Harry Blackburn (10)
Wallop CP School

Kennings Lion

Meat ripper
jungle prowler
mane swayer
day sleeper
deer killer
fur licker
tail flicker
night creeper
loud roarer
pride keeper
cub watcher.

Amy Donald (11)
Wallop CP School

Hot And Cold

Hot
Scalding, boiling,
burning, spitting, bubbling,
blistering boiling - ice-cold
freezing, frosty water
Iced, chilled,
Cold.

Joseph Day (10)
Wallop CP School

Sea

Wet, wondrous,
crashing, sparkling, splashing,
tranquil, turquoise - barren, endless,
waving, swirling, blowing
sandy, bare,
Desert

Emily Whordley (10)
Wallop CP School

Kennings Dog

Carpet digger
Lap sitter
Stick fetcher
Home guarder
Child minder
Heavy breather
Loud snorer
Territory marker
Smelly dropper
Fast runner
Meat eater
Ball snatcher
Flea scratcher
Food gobbler
Good swimmer
Messy dribbler
Vacuum cleaner
Basket sleeper.

Adam Bate (11)
Wallop CP School

Kennings Monkey

Tree swinger
Banana eater
Baby heater
Leaf leaper
Tree sleeper
Loud speaker
Food seeker
Moon howler
Tail flicker
Fur licker
Claw tapper
Night prowler

Ashley Baxter (11)
Wallop CP School

What's For Lunch?

Tickly tiger
Ate a spider,
Slithery snake
Bakes a cake.
Clucky chicken
Lollipop licken'
Farmer's dog,
Bites a frog.
Goldfish
Special dish,
White dove
Ice cream, love.
Blue whale
Bread stale,
Skunk, smelly
Eats wobbly jelly.
Grizzly bear
Eats a pear,
Now it's time to go back home
And enter the 'sleep-in' zone,
It's been a sunny day with lots of light,
But now it's time to say goodnight.

Annabel Dahne (9)
Wallop CP School

The Wind

The wind is lashing
And it is crashing.
The wind can be warm,
And it takes many forms.
The wind is playing,
Trees start swaying.
The wind sings a song,
But it never lasts long.

Anna Hibberd (7)
Wallop CP School

Kennings Leopard

Shadow sleeker
Food seeker
Animal catcher
Cat stretcher
Vegetable hater
Determined hunter
Kitten feeder
Long time sleeper
Tree climber
Perfect timer
Meat eater
Human scratcher
Leopard dreamer.

Cecilia King (10)
Wallop CP School

My Best Friend

My best friend is a real pain
My best friend is really insane
One day she went blue
Turned into a kangaroo
And hopped all the way over to Spain.

Jessica Fenton (11)
Wallop CP School

Tigers

Brightly striped creatures,
Roam on the wet jungle floors,
Watching for its prey.

Katherine Shadwell (11)
Wallop CP School

Kennings Dog

Tail slicker
Face licker
Bone eater
Furry heater
Basket sleeper
Bone keeper
Night walker
Dog talker
Fur stroker
Playing poker
Dig holes
Kill moles
Cat chaser
Dog racer.

Christopher Gallop (11)
Wallop CP School

Kennings Whale

Sea jumper
Boat thumper
Tail flicker
Fish licker
Fin lover
Wet cover
Sea swimmer
Life dimmer
Fish eater
People seeker.

Chloe Wood (10)
Wallop CP School

Kennings Parrot

Loud talker
Noisy squawker
Seed eater
Wing beater
Fruit squeezer
Jungle screecher
Sky flyer
Getting higher

Andrew Brotherwood (11)
Wallop CP School

The Wind

The wind will blast
It will never last
Get your kite
Take it for a flight
Here comes the sun
For everyone.

Jack Brown (7)
Wallop CP School

Summer

Hot, dry
burning, steaming, dehydrating,
warm, breezy - white, cold,
freezing, snowing, blowing,
snowman, ice,
Winter.

Jessica Malcolm (10)
Wallop CP School

Kennings Cat

Fur licker
Tail flicker
Pole scratcher
Mouse catcher
Risk taker
Mischief maker
High jumper
Ball thumper.

Robin Cook (11)
Wallop CP School

The Weather

The wind creeps
Sometimes peeps
The wind is like sea
Crashing and roaring
And clapping like thunder.

James Scott (8)
Wallop CP School

The Koala

As it gobbles leaves,
Safely in trees from danger,
Beautiful soft fur,
Crawling safely up a tree,
I hope it doesn't eat me.

Kieron Grist (11) & Andrew
Wallop CP School

The Weather

The wind lashes, lash, lash, lash,
And the rain crashes, crash, crash, crash.

The rain is getting really fast,
But I just don't want it to last.

The wind is howling,
And the rain is growling.

The wind is lashing,
And the trees are crashing.

The children all snuggled up in their beds,
And laid down their weary heads.

There was a sudden strike of lightning,
And it was very frightening.

Alexandra Bryony Sears (7)
Wallop CP School

Kennings Bear

Human scratcher
Animal catcher
Flesh tearer
Prey scarer
Roar maker
Ground shaker
Meat eater
Cave sleeper
Fierce grizzler
Scary hisser
Claw attacker
Body hacker.

Kate O'Brien (10)
Wallop CP School

The Weather

The rain was slithering down my window,
There was a shower last night.

There was a loud boom which was thunder,
Last night there was thunder near our house,
It wasn't very scary, not even for a mouse.

The clouds burst open suddenly,
The thunder was roaring like a lion.

The wind was howling,
And thunder growling.

The wind was crashing,
The wind was swaying to make the trees dance.

There was a gale,
The sun was shining like a lance.

The tornado was spinning,
The wind was winning,
But I was clinging.

Emma Sophie Blackburn (8)
Wallop CP School

The Weather

The wind was gusting through the trees
Through the branches and over the leaves.

Wind is strong like a lion
Sounding like a siren.

Thunder is like cymbals crashing like pinballs
The wind roars, sometimes soars.

Lightning flashes
The wind sometimes lashes.

Rory Wood (7)
Wallop CP School

Kennings Budgie

Wing flapper
Feather dropper
Seed eater
Water spiller
Fast flyer
Millet nibbler
Noisy squawker
Feathered flyer.

Christopher Burden (10)
Wallop CP School

Snow

Snow is very cold,
It goes brown when it's old.
Now everyone plays with snow,
I like it and so do you!
Oh I like how we play,
Snowball fights every day.
We play in the snow, hip, hip, hooray,
Do you think I like today?

Kara Hind (7)
Wallop CP School

Limerick

There was an old lady from Spain
Who lived in a sugar cane
The sugar was so sweet
She went tweet, tweet
Again and again and again.

Sophie Johnson (10)
Wallop CP School

Kennings Dog

Cat chaser
Bone placer
Biscuit eater
Warm seater
Paw licker
Tail flicker
Rat trapper.

Jason Dibble (10)
Wallop CP School

Kennings Bird

Wing flapper
Feather dropper
Seed eater
Noisy squawker
Fast flyer
Water spitter
Perch sitter.

Luke Bulpitt (11)
Wallop CP School

Limerick

There was a man from Dudley
Who was in a bed all snugly
He went downstairs
And found some bears
They looked all cute and cuddly.

Oliver Yates & Adam Bate (11)
Wallop CP School

My Pets

Gerbils jump,
Gerbils chew,
Gerbils love to squeak a tune.

Dogs jump,
Dogs chew,
Dogs love to bark a tune.

Fish jump,
Fish swim,
Fish love to bubble a tune.

Cats jump,
Cats chew,
Cats love to miaow a tune.

Animals are sweet and so are you,
So come and join our animal zoo!

Lauren Wood (11)
Wildground Junior School

My Gerbil

She's soft and black and round,
She burrows underground,
She escapes in one big bound,
Without making the slightest sound.

My fish swim around,
In the tank all day long,
And as for the fish food,
Well, it really pongs.

The foxes in the garden,
Waiting to pounce on their prey,
As the ground begins to harden,
The victim flies away.

Stephanie Randell (11)
Wildground Junior School

Jokes Of Valentine's Day

Roses are red,
My feet are blue,
I've got the hiccups,
And the rats ate the stew.

Mike's lost his flowers,
For his valentine,
Jody's very happy,
For the first time.

John's got a lady,
So a card is today's make,
Well, today is the day,
So he baked a cake.

Peter's had a girlfriend,
For two and a half years,
Now it's come to the end,
It will all end in tears.

Josie Myers (8)
Wildground Junior School

My Cat Maddy

My cat,
Is not very fat,
Her name is Maddy,
She is not a baddy.
She is my best friend,
She can really bend,
This is my cat,
I would not prefer a bat.

Kailey Hole (11)
Wildground Junior School

Little Hedgehog

I'm a little hedgehog who has a lot of prickles,
And when my mummy kisses me she always says it tickles.
When I go to bed, I'm always a funny shape,
So I have to stick my prickles down with Sellotape.
When my daddy cuddles me, he makes me feel so warm,
He makes me feel so cuddly, he also makes me yawn.
When I went to bed I had a great surprise,
I woke up one morning and saw the sunrise.
It was all sorts of colours, red and yellow too,
It made me feel so wonderful, imagine what it could do for you.

Nicole Perry (11)
Wildground Junior School

Happy

Happiness is purple like big juicy grapes
It tastes like vanilla ice cream
It smells like hot pork pies from the oven
It looks like my mum at home
It sounds like birds singing in the trees
It feels like being cuddled up in my duvet in bed.

Laura Thurston (8)
Wildground Junior School

The Ballerina Bear

I have a special little loved . . . ballerina bear.
I take her to my dance class, then back home again.
Her friend is Lucy doll.
She's my sweet little ballerina bear.

Holly Penny (9)
Wildground Junior School

Brothers

Up in my room,
Watching TV,
When my brother came upstairs,
To annoy me.
'What are you doing?
What is this ad?'
'Get out of my room!' I say,
'Before I shout Mum and Dad!'
Then he says, 'Chill it girl!'
And walks over to my windowsill.
Soon he rolls onto the floor,
Out of my room, out of my door,
Then I sigh and think again . . .
What else are brothers for?

Ellen Powell (10)
Wildground Junior School

My Mum

My mum wakes me up.
I'd better get ready and I'd better hurry up.

I'm running home to have my tea,
I'm in a state,
Because if I'm late -
My mum will be cross with me.

My mum smacks my bum.
When she cooks my tea, it tastes very yum, yum, *yum!*
She tickles my tummy when I'm feeling glum.
Oh I do so love my mum!

Jessica Maunder (9)
Wildground Junior School

A Silent Night

A silent night
While children sleep
Babies cry
And home cats creep.

Shadows of trees
By the moonlight
And owls emerge
For their midnight flight.

When the sun rises
And the birds begin to sing
Children wake up as their alarm clocks ring.

Bethany Hibberd (10)
Wildground Junior School

Night-Time

I like the night-time,
Looking at the stars,
I try to catch a glimpse,
Of Pluto, Venus or Mars.

'Cause everything's so peaceful,
Right here where I lie,
Thinking and wondering,
Looking at the sky.

Shannen Sultana (10)
Wildground Junior School

The Months

January brings New Year
everyone goes to cheer

February brings Valentine's love
while the dove flies above

March brings life to the trees
leaves flow in the breeze

April brings the Easter bunny
it does look really funny

May brings heavy rain
and goes to flood the plain

June brings a summer sun
we all have a lot of fun

Hot July brings no more school
more playing in the pool

August brings my birthday
I go and say hip, hip, hooray

Warm September brings back to school
no more visiting Uncle Paul

Fresh October brings Hallowe'en
I am getting really keen

Dull November brings evenings dark
no more playing in the park

Chill December brings icy cold
everything goes mouldy mould.

Michael Quinn (8)
Wildground Junior School

Pet Shop

P is for parrot pestering people.
E is for eel electrocuting everything.
T is for tarantula tickling toes.

S is for snake slithering slyly.
H is for hare hopping happily.
O is for ostrich on odd skinny legs.
P is for pet shop staff darting out the door.

Chelsea Penny (10)
Wildground Junior School

The Zoo

T is for tiger prowling about.
H is for hippo, greedy for food.
E is for elephant with a long, wavy trunk.

Z is for zebra, 'I am not buckaroo.'
O is for ostrich, 'I am better than you.'
O is for otter, 'I am a very good swimmer.'

Rebecca Mole (11)
Wildground Junior School

Snake

S lithering across the ground
N asty to its prey
A dders are snakes
K illing their victims
E mpty stomachs? Never.

Amy Benham (11)
Wildground Junior School

Happiness

Happiness is blue like the sea.
It tastes like milkshake.
It looks like having fun.
It feels like being in a car.
It smells like new clean clothes.

Ben Fusedale (7)
Wildground Junior School

Sadness

Sadness is a whale lost in the sea,
Sadness is a bare display with no one looking after it,
Like a slow movement in my tummy ready to move somewhere else,
Like tears rolling down my cheeks,
Like people sitting in the street alone,
That's what sadness is.

Eleanor Watson (8)
Wildground Junior School

Why?

Why is the sky blue?
Why do we have night and day?
Why do we live in the wilderness?
So now I wonder why.

Catherine Hoare (11)
Wildground Junior School

My Cat Smudge

My cat Smudge,
Eats all my fudge.

He curls up at night.
His white fur on his neck is so bright.

He has a black nose.
He lays on all my clothes.

My cat Smudge likes chicken, turkey and beef.
Who ate my fudge? Oh Smudge, you little thief.

Catriona O'Brien (8)
Wildground Junior School

Love

Love is like a heart beating fast,
Love is like a best friend,
Love is like a boy's and girl's heart,
Love is like an angel blessing you,
Love is like a rose,
Love is like a rose that never dies,
Now you know what love is
And now you can go and love someone.
Good luck.

Louise Holloway (9)
Wildground Junior School